William Tallack

**Thomas Shillitoe**

The Quaker Missionary and Temperance Pioneer

William Tallack

**Thomas Shillitoe**
*The Quaker Missionary and Temperance Pioneer*

ISBN/EAN: 9783337405137

Printed in Europe, USA, Canada, Australia, Japan

Cover: Foto ©Lupo / pixelio.de

More available books at **www.hansebooks.com**

# THOMAS SHILLITOE,

THE

## QUAKER MISSIONARY

AND

## TEMPERANCE PIONEER.

BY

## WILLIAM TALLACK,

*Author of "Peter Bedford, the Spitalfields Philanthropist," &c.*

LONDON:

S. W. PARTRIDGE, 9, PATERNOSTER ROW.

—

1867.

# PREFACE.

A DESIRE has often been expressed for a popular and portable memoir of the late Thomas Shillitoe, a man of whom it may be truly affirmed that he was one of the most remarkable of modern missionaries and philanthropists. The writer of the present life has sought to furnish such a memoir, and in it he has embodied many personal reminiscences of its subject, communicated by surviving friends, and has also availed himself of various unpublished documents, kindly lent by a member of Mr. Shillitoe's family.

The principal aim has been to promote an increased interest in the great Christian principles and objects of social progress, which were so intimately associated with the efforts of the good man whose career is here described. Frequent allusions have also been made to kindred labours and experiences.

*Crown 8vo, with a Portrait, price 2s. 6d., cloth.*

# PETER BEDFORD,

## THE SPITALFIELDS PHILANTHROPIST.

CONTAINING AN INTERESTING ACCOUNT OF HIS LABOURS IN THE
METROPOLIS, ESPECIALLY AMONG THE THIEVES.

———

### By WILLIAM TALLACK.

# CONTENTS.

## CHAPTER I.

### GENERAL ASPECT OF HIS LIFE.

## CHAPTER II.

### YOUTH AND EARLY MANHOOD.

## CHAPTER III.

### HIS HOME MISSIONS AND ORDINARY MINISTRY.

## CHAPTER IV.

### HIS FOREIGN MISSIONS.

## CHAPTER V.

### FURTHER FOREIGN MISSIONS—RUSSIA AND AMERICA.

## CHAPTER VI.

### VISITS TO SOVEREIGNS AND INFLUENTIAL PERSONS.

## CHAPTER VII.

### EFFORTS IN PROMOTION OF TEMPERANCE.

# THOMAS SHILLITOE,

# QUAKER MISSIONARY.

## CHAPTER I.

### GENERAL ASPECT OF HIS LIFE.

A UNIVERSAL PHILANTHROPIST—AN EARLY LABOURER FOR TEMPERANCE, PRISON REFORM, ABOLITION OF SLAVERY, AND SABBATH OBSERVANCE—HIS STRONG SENSE OF INDIVIDUAL RESPONSIBILITY—HIS DEEP CHRISTIAN EARNESTNES —WEAKNESSES AND STRUGGLES.

ALTHOUGH comparatively unknown to fame, even amongst the religious world, Thomas Shillitoe may, without exaggeration, be described as one of the most remarkable men of modern times. A member of one of the smallest sects in Christendom, and peculiarly destitute of any special educational or social advantages, he lived a life of wonderful energy as *a universal philanthropist* and as a Christian minister of almost apostolic activity.

B

Long before the establishment of the great philanthropic organizations of the present day, he had vigorously devoted himself to the advocacy of their respective principles, and, throughout his career, vigilantly seized opportunities of urging their importance upon persons in influential positions. Almost a quarter of a century before the formation of Temperance Societies, he laboured assiduously to mitigate the evils of drunkenness. Independently of Prison-Reform Associations, he made strenuous exertions on behalf of the religious and temporal interests of prisoners at home and abroad. Whilst Slavery was still generally countenanced by Christian nations, and even by the British Government in its colonial dependencies, Thomas Shillitoe, at personal risk, pleaded with slave owners on their plantations, for the oppressed bondsmen. And, many years previous to the modern associated efforts for promoting the reverent observance of the Lord's day, this unwearied man visited the chief sovereigns and dignitaries of Europe, in whose presence he boldly set forth the spiritual and social evils of Sabbath desecration.

Whilst thus engaged in so great a variety of benevolent services, he was equally indefatigable in his labours as a minister of the Gospel. We should rather say that he considered all the above objects as being subordinate parts of his ministry, and not merely collateral or independent matters. Knowing how inseparably man's spiritual destinies are connected with his temporal circumstances and material surroundings, Thomas Shillitoe regarded physical and social hindrances to religious progress as parts of the hostile army against which it was the duty of the Church militant to wage uncompromising warfare, and in her ranks he was a faithful soldier. Yet not altogether can he be said to have served in her ranks. Shillitoe, like Whitfield and many others, was not formed for easy co-operation with fellow-workers.

His individuality was so strongly marked, his opinions so decided, and his constitutional temperament so sensitive, and at times even morbidly nervous, that he found the greater freedom and success in a large measure of lonely effort. Thus most of his numerous journeys were performed without a companion, a very unusual course with ministers of the denomination to which he belonged. In reading his letters and addresses, the constant manifestation of an innocent egotism is very striking. The pronouns " I," " my," " me," crowd his memoranda; but only in the humble simplicity of a person whose very soul was permeated by an abiding sense of the solemnity of his individual responsibility to one Divine Master.

This strong sense of individual responsibility is the key not only to the extraordinary career of Shillitoe, but also to the very large comparative influence which the exceedingly small sect of the Friends has exercised upon the world. That a body of Christians numbering, in the United Kingdom, less than fifteen thousand (less altogether than the members of other denominations often included in the population of a single town), should have succeeded, as they have done, in being recognized as taking a foremost place of influence in the accomplishment of almost every great philanthropic and progressive movement of the age, and in having anticipated most of such movements amongst themselves, indicates some very powerful basis of action. That basis is one early inculcated upon the true Friend—the sense of an inalienable, untransferable responsibility to his God and Saviour, an obligation to serve Him as one who must give an account for himself to God, and who may not rely even upon the Church or upon her officers for any relief from that awful responsibility.

This feeling of personal duty to God and to Christ, urged on Thomas Shillitoe through the arduous career which he accomplished. If he met with difficulties and discouragements, he looked to his Master for their removal or conquest. Feeling his own entire weakness, he prayed the more earnestly and perseveringly for the presence of the energies imparted by God's Holy Spirit. Taking the Bible as the chart of his life's voyage, and imploring the influences of the Spirit as an impelling and sustaining power, he lived his earthly term of discipleship and service. And looking beyond Time into the invisible but permanent realities of the future Kingdom, he derived an animating steadying power which rendered him indifferent to human honour or celebrity, and sustained him in a quiet unostentatious perseverance to the end.

He indeed persevered strenuously and lived vigilantly; for to him the Christian's prospect was one of intense seriousness. He believed firmly his Lord's assertions, "Straight is the gate, and narrow is the way, which leadeth unto life, and few there be that find it." "Many, I say unto you, will seek to enter in and shall not be able." He read in the glorious descriptions of the future New Jerusalem and its kingdom, recorded by the Prophets and Apostles so repeatedly, the strict requirements of faithful obedience, obtainable by prayer, through Christ's grace, and hence he felt it necessary to "give diligence," and to "earnestly contend for the faith once delivered to the saints." He felt that, both as to himself and to others, the glorious gift of eternal life through Christ, was promised only conditionally, and only to the believer. He deemed the Christian course a race for a prize, to be won with difficulty ; and, like the Apostle, the tenour of his preaching continually was, "So run that ye may obtain." This strong sense of the serious business of salvation pervaded him to the last, and on his death-bed (after a peculiarly saintly life) he exclaimed, "Oh, that I could get within the pearl gates—just within the pearl gates. I feel I have nothing to depend upon but the mercies of God in Christ Jesus. I do not rely for salvation upon any merits of my own; all my own works are as filthy rags : my faith is in the merits of Christ Jesus, and in the offering He made for us. I trust my past sins are all forgiven me—that they have been washed away by the blood of Christ, who died for my sins. It is mercy I want, and mercy I have."

Thus, every way, Thomas Shillitoe was a soldier of the Cross—his life an arduous endeavour after the prize of eternal life, for himself and for others—a prize precious and costly, inasmuch as it was purchased only by the blood and sufferings of the Lord Jesus Christ, and only to be qualified for by the gifts of the Holy Spirit which His death procured for men.

That a life comprising so many striking incidents as that of Thomas Shillitoe should not be known in general beyond the narrow circle of his small sect, is not surprising when his humility and retiring quietude are considered.

He counted it a small matter to receive honour from men who would soon pass away. If he could win a place in the future Kingdom at "the coming of our Lord Jesus Christ with all His saints," that was the only thing worth his anxiety and labour. In this characteristic feature of his life he resembled thousands of good men in all ages of the Jewish and Christian church. The prayerful work of "laying up treasure in Heaven" was his desire. When he found it necessary to come out publicly in Christian effort, he boldly did so, but was glad to get back into private life again. And during his travels he felt a special interest in seeking out and consoling persons who, like himself, had their hopes and aspirations directed with simplicity toward God and Christ. He remembered the hidden but Divinely reserved seven thousand who had not bowed the knee to Baal, but on whom the Lord's good pleasure rested, in old time, and the countless number of good Jews and Christians ever since, unknown to biographers, or to the public mind, but "whose record is on high," and whose names are written in the Book of Life, of the coming era, when they will "be had in everlasting remembrance," and be blessed with the raised saints of the Kingdom in "the new heavens and new earth," which are to succeed this present dispensation.

It is but fair to add, that whilst conspicuous as a missionary and philanthropist, the subject of this memoir was also characterized by a full share of the frailties and imperfections common to humanity. Thus he was often impetuous and irritable, sometimes obstinate, occasionally uncharitable, and always more or less nervous and eccentric.

But these weaknesses, some of which were the results of his physical constitution, render his persevering, prayerful, and laborious life, the more instructive and exemplary. Mere innocence may be exhibited by childhood and infancy, or even by the gentle irrational lamb and peaceful dove. But righteousness, holiness, and advanced progress towards perfection, are only developed amid conflict, temptation, and prayerful resistance. Hence the beauty and interest of such biographies as those of Jacob, David, Peter, John, and Paul, whose struggles and imperfections are recorded in the pages of inspiration, as instructive proofs that their graces were gifts from above, and developed, amid conflict, by the operations of Divine visitation.

Thomas Shillitoe was a good man, but also one of many weaknesses, and to have ignored these would have greatly lessened the value of his peculiarly instructive life.

# CHAPTER II.

## YOUTH AND EARLY MANHOOD.

CHILDHOOD AND PARENTAL CARE—THREE YEARS IN A PUBLIC-
HOUSE—DEPRAVITY AND VIOLENCE OF THE EIGHTEENTH
CENTURY—A GROCER'S APPRENTICE AT WAPPING AND PORTS-
MOUTH—RETURNS TO LONDON—JOINS THE FRIENDS—DIF-
FICULTIES IN CONSEQUENCE—HIS INTEGRITY AMID SUR-
ROUNDING COMPLIANCE WITH THE SPIRIT OF THE TIMES—
QUITS A BANK TO BECOME A SHOEMAKER—TRIALS—HIS PRO-
SPECTS BRIGHTEN—SETTLES AT TOTTENHAM—MARRIAGE—
GRADUALLY ACQUIRES PROPERTY—HIS ULTIMATE RETIREMENT
FROM BUSINESS TO DEVOTE HIMSELF TO THE SERVICE OF GOD.

THOMAS SHILLITOE was born in London in May, 1754, a period when the Dead Sea lifelessness of "the leaden age of England," the eighteenth century, was being in many places roused into an unwonted excitement by the preaching of Wesley and Whitfield. He furnishes us with an illustration of the constantly observed fact that "As the twig is bent, the tree 's inclined," and that personal piety and usefulness are largely dependent on early parental care and godly nurture amid the critical years when abiding habits, for good or for evil, are usually formed. His father was Librarian of Gray's Inn. Both father and mother were earnestly desirous of bringing up their children in a virtuous life. They belonged to the Established Church, and habitually inculcated a due observance of its rites and services on the members of their family. And not merely so, but it was their endeavour, as Thomas tells us, to train him and the other children "in every moral duty." This speaks well for their seriousness and sincerity as the heads of a household.

There may be an outward profession of religion, and regular church or chapel-going; but all will be in vain, unless truth, kindliness, honesty, industry, and other "moral duties" give evidence of the energizing presence of a Christianity which affects the heart and conduct. That special care in these respects was extended towards the young Shillitoes is further evidenced by the record that they were "kept close indoors, seldom being allowed to go into the company of other children except at school."

When Thomas was about twelve years old, his father found himself unable to continue his duties at Gray's Inn, through the infirmities of approaching age, and therefore, with a view to an "easy life," started as an innkeeper at Islington, as landlord of "The Three Tuns." But, as in many cases since, the life of a publican was not found to be conducive either to repose, to morals, or to real advantage. After three or four years spent in his new occupation, poor Mr. Shillitoe had in one way and another run through his little property, and was glad to resume a quiet life at Gray's Inn once more, as a supernumerary or semi-retired official.

It was well for Thomas that his father did not continue in "the public line," for it was already producing a mischievous effect upon his hitherto carefully guarded morals. He was considered old enough to help in the business, and

was required to serve out liquor and assist generally. Sundays in particular were very busy days with him. But his parents still required his attendance at church; and it is creditable to them and to their son, that the latter records his remembrance of the still abiding feelings of reverence with which at this period of his life he used to kneel down in public prayer and confession on these occasions. We may believe that, after the past years of earnest endeavour for a godly life, Mr. Shillitoe and his son would listen with mingled feelings to the clergyman's frequent utterance of the suggestive words—" Wherefore let us beseech Him to grant us true repentance and his Holy Spirit, *that those things may please Him which we do at this present*, and that the rest of our life hereafter may be pure and holy, so that at the last we may come to his eternal joy through Jesus Christ our Lord." As it was an age of drunkenness and profligacy, and as young Thomas tells us, he was " exposed to all sorts of company and allowed to ramble the village unprotected both by day and late of an evening, carrying out beer to the customers," it may be presumed that he was in imminent danger of losing the freshness of " the dew of his youth." But happily the exposure did not continue long enough to undo the work of his guarded and well-instructed childhood. The father's failure was the son's gain, as it led to his being apprenticed to a more respectable line of life, that of a grocer, at Wapping.

It may appear strange to the reader, that in the allusion to his public-house life, just quoted, Thomas speaks of Islington as " The Village." But that which is now a populous portion of the great metropolis was then a small and straggling suburb. Between it and the City were gardens and fields. At the period of Thomas's boyhood, "The Angel" at Islington was a famous rural tavern whither the citizens repaired on summer afternoons and evenings to enjoy themselves. So miserably inadequate was the constabulary of those days, that highway robberies and murderous assaults were everyday occurrences even in and around London. Hence parties were formed, every half-hour, of citizens returning from the Angel to the city, who came home in numbers united for mutual protection. This was the period when Britain was engaged in almost perpetual warfare with other countries for "the balance of power," whilst her own home administration was in an unparalleled condition of disorganization and corruption. Horace Walpole speaks of the then dangers of English locomotion thus—"One is forced to travel, even at noon, as if one were going to battle." Mr. Andrews, in his work on "the Eighteenth Century," graphically describes such incidents as bludgeon fights and fatal assaults which not unfrequently occurred in Fleet Street and the Strand; highwaymen attacked chaises in Piccadilly, and escaped by riding over the "watchmen." The mails were robbed by wholesale.

Meanwhile on Hounslow Heath, Hampstead, and such open spaces, the "deterrent" gibbet was displayed incessantly, but only to be regarded as a scarecrow by ruffians of whom the authorities were afraid. In his work on "Crime," Mr. Frederic Hill records the following incident :—"An elderly lady with whom I was well acquainted, and who has not long been dead, had occasion on the wedding excursion of a friend to whom she had

acted as bridesmaid, to pass in the dusk of the evening
over Hounslow Heath. As they approached a mound
they saw, *under three gibbets that had been erected there*,
a group of men whom the travelling party suspected to
be highwaymen, and they therefore proceeded immediately to conceal their money and jewels. Before they
could effect their purpose, however, the highwaymen,
for such they were, presented themselves masked, and,
with pistols in hand, succeeded in obtaining possession
of several watches, and nearly forty pounds in money,
before they were alarmed by the approach of other carriages and obliged to decamp."

In the earlier portion of the eighteenth century there
had been formed, amongst the young " bloods," a systematic association for conducting street outrages. Respectable citizens were surrounded by these wild fellows,
and obliged to dance round at their pleasure, obedience
being enforced by pricking their legs with the points of
swords worn by the young " gentlemen." Often worse
followed, noses were slit, skulls cracked, and limbs
broken. Long after Shillitoe's boyhood astounding social
evils were prevalent in the metropolis and throughout the
country ; and yet there are still persons who recur with
sentimental regret to the " Good old days of George the
Third," those days without order, without legal justice,
without gas, without rapid coaches, to say nothing of
railways and telegraph ; days when the pulpit was asleep,
the bar and even the bench corrupt, the legislature openly
purchaseable, and the populace in a general condition of
ignorance, brutality, and moral indifference. Men were at
any time liable to be torn away from their families by

savage press-gangs; whole crews of honest sailors, just returned from a long voyage, were sometimes obliged to fight for their liberty with the King's officers. Yet a favourite tune was "Britons never will be slaves." Duelling and fighting were universally in vogue. Drunkenness was more prevalent than at any preceding period. It was inscribed in large letters outside the publican's houses, at this period, that persons might get drunk for a penny, dead drunk for twopence, and have straw for nothing, liquor at that time being remarkably cheap and untaxed. All around the coast smuggling afforded a livelihood to thousands. It is recorded that on one occasion a cavalcade of some ten waggons, each drawn by four horses, and all laden with "run" goods, was escorted safely to London by smugglers. On entering the City a pitched battle ensued, in which the revenue officers were obliged to retreat, and the smugglers succeeded in safely housing their spoil. Meanwhile the judges at the Old Bailey and elsewhere perseveringly hung men, women, and children by the half-dozen and dozen at a time; but the evils of the time continued as bad as ever.

Such were the days of Shillitoe's boyhood; and it is no wonder that his parents, when able, should have kept him and his brothers "close indoors," except when at school.

Thomas was sixteen years of age when he removed from Islington to Wapping. But at the latter place he speedily found fresh cause to deplore the mischiefs of intemperance. He had barely been twelve months in the grocery trade when his master, whose drinking habits had

latterly increased to an extent which precluded his pros-
perity, was compelled to relinquish his business. But
having relatives at Portsmouth he removed thither and
resumed the same occupation, taking his apprentice,
Thomas, with him. The latter now found things worse
than ever. Surrounded by profligate scenes of the worst
description, he shrunk with horror from the frequent contact with vicious and degraded persons which was now
forced upon him, as his master's shop was situated in the
lowest part of the town. It is greatly to the youth's
credit that, in order to counteract the contaminating influences to which he was daily exposed, he sought to find
virtuous companions from whose society he might derive
some confirmation in his honest desires after a life of
integrity and piety. Both at Wapping and Portsmouth
he succeeded in forming some useful acquaintance of this
description. But beyond all other means of preservation
at this critical period, Thomas ascribes his safety to the
continued renewal of serious impressions in his heart, by
the visitations of the Holy Spirit of the Lord who had
graciously watched over his childhood, and who had surrounded him with a peculiar measure of parental care and
protection.

Feeling from time to time these freshened constraints
towards a life of godliness and peace, Thomas became at
length so thoroughly dissatisfied with his position at
Portsmouth that he wrote to his parents entreating them
to procure his release from his indentures. This was
eventually accomplished, and returning to London he once
more entered a grocery business, but this time as an assistant to a sober, God-fearing tradesman, whom Thomas

mentions as having been "a great help to me." He was
a regular attendant of public worship and encouraged his
assistant to accompany him, taking a sincere interest in
his religious and moral improvement. After three years
spent in this quiet situation, Thomas became acquainted
with a young man, a distant relative, some of whose con-
nections were Quakers, and who was in the habit of
attending the meetings of that denomination. Thither he
persuaded Thomas to accompany him. This soon became
a regular habit ; but Thomas frankly records : "My
motive for this change was not a pure one ; my chief
inducement being to meet my young relation and afterwards go home to dine with him ; his acquaintance causing
me to neglect the attendance of a place of worship the remaining part of the day, which had been my uniform practice
for the last three years. My new companion also took
me to the most fashionable tea-gardens and other places
of public resort, where we spent the afternoon and at
times the evening.

After more than a year of this life Shillitoe's mind
became very uneasy. Conscience smote him for his retro-
grade habits on the Sabbath, and he was brought into
serious considerations of his ingratitude to God who had
followed him thus far with his protection and gracious
invitations to piety. Thomas, whose youthful seriousness
had never wholly passed away, now resolutely endeavoured
to commit himself to a decided course. Acknowledging
the mercy of God's renewed visitation to his soul, he
earnestly prayed that his Heavenly Father would now
establish him permanently in a righteous course, that He
would never again leave him or permit the enemy of his

soul to lead him astray, and that whatever discipline might be needful to secure life-long faithfulness might not be withheld. These prayers were graciously and permanently answered. From that time forward Thomas's life was an uninterrupted advance in godliness. Never again was he prevailed upon by temptation, to forsake either the profession or the practice of a decidedly religious life. And henceforth he diligently sought to manifest his fidelity to his Lord by act and endeavour as well as by the profession of the Christian name.

Although he had been induced to attend the worship of the Friends from motives which were not really religious, and although for some time he does not appear to have derived benefit from that attendance, yet he gradually became impressed with a conviction that it would be well for him to become an adherent of a denomination whose worship afforded such peculiar incitements to reverent individual prayer and meditation, and whose general conduct was characterized by peculiar sobriety and straightforward, unambitious rectitude. Henceforth, and for the remainder of his life, Thomas Shillitoe became a member of the Society of Friends.

But, in arriving at this conclusion, he had a painful and very trying ordeal to pass through. His parents, although, as we have seen, serious and careful persons, entertained a decided dislike of Quakerism, and manifested much opposition to their son's union with that sect. In common with many others, they had probably imbibed very mistaken opinions relative to the Friends, who in the eighteenth century had greatly fallen away from the fervour and proselytizing activity of their founders and predecessors

Further, the absence of the Holy Scriptures from their worship, and the great importance which at that period the Friends attached to certain traditional outward observances, had given rise to an incorrect but wide-spread impression that they rejected the Bible, and were not orthodox in their views of Christ's divinity or in their desire to obey His sacred commands. The latter charges have often been alleged against them by their opponents, but not by those who truly understand them. In the present day Quakerism has thrown off the slumbers and formalism of its eighteenth century life, in good degree at least ; and its followers are now again, like their energetic founders, manifesting an active and philanthropic interest in the spiritual and social advance of their fellow-men, and a clearer and more unmistakable reverence for the Holy Scriptures, which are the chief channel and most honoured instrument for the operations of the Divine Spirit who inspired them. Thomas Shillitoe himself was one of the very first persons who infused a new life into the denomination to which he now committed himself.

But, for the present at least, he failed to convince his parents that the step taken by him was a progressive one. They grieved over him as forsaking the path in which they had carefully trained him, and in which certainly God had blessed him with much approval of his youthful faithfulness to the Church of which he had been hitherto a member. We should rather say that he merely quitted one department of the indivisible Church of Christ for another department. There is but one true Church—the Zion of the Lord Jesus. But, like Mount Zion itself, though presenting certain grand outlines visible to all and recognized by all who approach it, yet it is many-sided, and some of its aspects vary considerably from others.

Shillitoe swerved not at all from his boyhood's aspiration to "go up to the mountain of the Lord;" but it was given him to see that it would be attended with manifold advantages, for him to select a path thitherward, hitherto untrodden by himself and wholly strange to his parents. God seemed to be thus calling him, and humbly, but decisively, he obeyed.

His training in one section of the Church and his subsequent union with another, gave him more enlarged views as to the equal godliness of Christians holding very different opinions on some religious questions. He was thus aided to understand the sacred assertion—" There are diversities of gifts, but the same Spirit. And there are differences of administrations, but the same Lord. And there are diversities of operations, but it is the same God, which worketh all in all " (1 Cor. xii. 4–6). Such an experience was peculiarly useful to one who was afterwards to become God's messenger to men of many outward forms of faith, speaking diverse tongues and belonging to races widely separated by ocean and continent.

Yet Thomas Shillitoe was henceforth a warmly attached adherent to his adopted section of the Church, feeling that the path which appeared specially adapted to him must be also specially pondered by him. His ascent of Mount Zion, his approach to the throne of the King whom he hoped and trusted one day to see manifest thereon, was to be by a path which he would carefully devote his attention to, apart from other means of access more suited to the diverse spiritual or mental constitution of others. For to one is given capacity and force of choice widely diverse from another, even as the alpine summit is attained in one manner by the eagle's flight, in another by the leaps of the bright-eyed chamois, and otherwise again by the persevering footstep of the human traveller.

The difficulties in which young Shillitoe was placed by the strong opposition of his parents to his union with the Friends attracted the sympathizing notice of a motherly member of that persuasion named Margaret Bell. She actively interested herself on his behalf, and soon procured him what she presumed would be a congenial situation as a clerk in a Quaker banking house in Lombard Street, where the young convert would be surrounded by associates of the same views as his own, and where his feelings would be sympathized with and appreciated. Thomas entered hopefully on his new situation, and devoted himself to a conscientious performance of its duties. But trials and disappointment awaited him even there. He had expected that, after the painful reminiscences of Islington, Wapping, and Portsmouth, a situation where his companions would be members of the sober sect of Friends must necessarily be in comparison a little guarded Eden, a place shielded from the temptations of a wicked world, and affording associations which, even more decidedly than the watchful oversight of his late worthy master, the church-going grocer, would be "a great help" to him. Alas! for human nature; Thomas speedily found it to be substantially the same, though, like the chamelion, presenting very various outward aspects. For a man to make a profession of special religious zeal whilst really following evil with as much zest as non-professors, is merely adding the greater sins of hypocrisy and falsehood.  Thomas grieved deeply to find in his new and demure looking companions persons who, when able to do so, freely indulged in gaiety and dissipation.  He sadly records of these, "many of them are as much given up to the world and its delusive pleasures as other professors of the Christian name."

It was further a matter of pain to him that his employers, the heads of the firm, yielded themselves and their subordinates to the demoralizing spirit of the day, inasmuch as they issued to their customers lottery tickets, which in the eighteenth century were so extensively patronized by the government.  Every form of gambling and betting characterized that wretched period, and pervaded all ranks of society.  Almost the whole time of the fashionable ladies was devoted to cards, masquerades, and routs.  Ladies, too, swore habitually "like troopers." One of Lord Mansfield's clerks declared of a certain one (in 1738)—"I could not make out, sir, who she was; but she swore so dreadfully that she must be a lady of quality!" This "lady" was the Duchess of Marlborough. Gentlemen of "quality" swore also, got drunk and betted almost universally.  A bet, which at the time attracted much attention, was entered into by Lord Rockingham and Lord Orford.  These noblemen staked five hundred guineas on the result of a journey to London from Norwich, to be performed by two batches of miserable birds— five turkeys and five geese.  Lord Orford won, for his geese arrived first.  The government fostered this gambling spirit officially by the issue of lottery tickets.  Thus tickets for a million pounds would be distributed, and eagerly purchased throughout the nation.  Of this one hundred thousand pounds would be apportioned in prizes, leaving a profit (less commission to agents) of nine hundred thousand. When the government thus led the way, and when even respectable Quaker houses undertook the distribution, it is no wonder that the populace rushed in multitudes after the "golden chances" so dispersed.

But the sterling piety of Thomas Shillitoe recoiled from this "going with a multitude to do evil." In him was a goodly measure of the spirit which animated of old "Athanasius against the world," and earlier still the three godly youths who unflinchingly refused to bow down to the golden image in the plain of Dura, notwithstanding it was that even " which Nebuchadnezzar the King had set up." Shillitoe was, in his way and generation, both a Daniel and an Athanasius. He had, probably, not been long enough amongst the Quakers to have read all the worthy deeds of George Fox and Edward Burrough, who, in the preceding century, were "firm as a rock and as stiff as a tree" in their "testimonies" against evil in high places. But Thomas strove for strength to bear his "testimony" too, even if it offended the dignity of the formal and stereotyped professors around him. He would be rather a Friend of the stamp of Fox, and would seek henceforth something deeper and higher than the merely traditional scrupulosities of his then degenerate successors. And he succeeded in his endeavours. But first he must leave Lombard Street.

Where next was he to go? What was he to do? Seriously and prayerfully he committed his way to the Lord, and craved that he might be guided aright. He reflected that he had now tried several situations, the public-house, the grocer's shop, and the bank. In each of these he had been diligent and active, but had suffered mainly from unavoidable association with others less conscientious than himself. It now appeared to him that it would be best to devote himself to some handicraft which he could pursue, if needful, in absolute solitude, or in which, at any rate, he might not be compelled always to be mixed up with the actions of uncongenial associates. The humble employment of shoemaking came before his mind, and after very serious consideration he determined to sacrifice worldly advantages for the prospects of quietude and independent exertion which that occupation promised. This resolution brought Thomas into fresh difficulties. His relatives, and even his kindly disposed Quaker friends, thought him foolish and deluded. Numerous were the remonstances urged against the adoption of the awl and last by a young man situated in a first-rate bank and with good prospects of probable advancement. Another difficulty arose from the humiliating change which would result from his having to relinquish the respectable appearance which he had now to maintain. For instance, he still wore a plain sword at his side, after the fashion of the day. But Thomas was ready to sacrifice all style and appearance to his conscientious scruples. His employers also appreciated his faithfulness, and would not at first entertain his proposal. Amid the conflict of advice and criticism Thomas again had recourse to his motherly friend Margaret Bell, who replied, with a woman's shrewdness, " The wise man says, ' in the multitude of counsellors there is safety,' but I say there often wants safety." She therefore advised him to look at the matter simply and mainly in its probable bearing on his religious advancement, and as in the sight of the Lord. From this point of view the course seemed plain. Thomas promptly decided, and resigned his clerkship accordingly.

His next step was to make an agreement with a shoemaker in Southwark, who undertook to teach him his handicraft in all its branches for the consideration of half the small sum which Thomas had managed to save. The latter perseveringly studied to become proficient in his new employment, but it was very humbling and unremunerative work for a long time. He records—"My little surplus of money wasted fast, and my earnings were very small, not allowing me more for the first twelve months than bread, cheese, and water, and sometimes bread only, to keep clear of getting into debt, which I carefully avoided. Sitting constantly on the seat at work made it hard for me, so that I might say I worked hard and fared hard. Many of my friends manifested a fear my health would suffer; but I soon became reconciled to the change in my diet, as did also my constitution." He adds that some of his friends used to remark that his cheerful and healthy looks reminded them of the countenance of Daniel and his companions after their vegetarian diet of pulse. On Sundays some of Thomas's acquaintances invited him to dinner, which afforded a welcome change from his scanty fare and unsocial occupation during the week.

Meanwhile he reflected with abiding satisfaction on the course he had committed himself to. Doubtless he would have uphill work at first, but eventually better days might

be hoped for.   He says,—" I trusted that if I kept close
to my good Guide in all my future steppings, He would
not fail so to direct me, that time would evince to my
friends, that I had not been deceived in the step I had
thus taken."   And so it proved.

Having mastered his craft, Thomas left his instructor in
the Borough, and took lodgings in the City, where he rapidly
obtained employment, especially from the Friends.   Things
were already looking bright, and it appeared likely that he
would soon be in possession of a promising business.   But
now a further trial overtook him.   His health failed; excessive weakness almost prostrated him, and the doctors
urged him to quit London.   It was not, however, necessary to go far.   At that time a numerous population of
Quakers inhabited Tottenham; to many of these Thomas
was well known, and thither he betook himself and resumed his shoe-business.   Here his health improved,
many customers came to him, two Quaker schools employed him, and he presently found himself obliged to
engage two journeymen to assist him.   Thomas was
twenty-three years old when he settled at Tottenham, in
1778, and from that time till his death, nearly sixty years
afterwards, in 1836, it was his home, with the exception
of several years spent with his children in Yorkshire, and
a similar period at Hitchin in Herts, when in advanced
life.   But the latter portion of his days were again spent
at Tottenham.

In allusion to the circumstances which led to his quitting
London for Tottenham, he says, "Thus does our great
almighty Care-taker, as we are willing to become subject
to his control and government, lead us about and in

various ways instruct us, by sickness and by health, by crosses and disappointments, that we of ourselves are poor feeble, fallible mortals, wholly at the disposal of, and under, His turning and overturning hand of power." Thomas throughout life habitually recognized the pointings of Providence, and implored, in frequent prayer, that the Lord would order his path aright, and truly be his Master and King. His constant committal of his path to God reminds us of the good man of ancient times, recorded in Holy Scripture as being "more honourable than his brethren;" and of whom it is added, "Jabez called on the God of Israel, saying, Oh, that thou wouldest bless me indeed, and enlarge my coast, and that thine hand might be with me, and that thou wouldest keep me from evil that it may not grieve me! And God granted him that which he requested." (1 Chronicles iv. 10.)

Like Jabez, Thomas Shillitoe desired to be "blessed *indeed*," not merely prospered in this life at the expense of his preparation for Christ's glorious kingdom, but so blessed that his final and everlasting happiness might be multiplied. He had already learned that many apparent blessings are often deadly curses; that, although competence, or a preservation from the severe temptations of poverty, is very desirable, yet that such a sense of independence as may lead to a forgetfulness of God, and to the neglect of His work and service, often kills the soul and entails the forfeiture of "the good things which God hath prepared for them that love Him." He had seen that, to the young especially, it is cruelty, instead of kindness, to bring them up in idleness and prosperous carelessness, instead of a participation in the healthful exercise of useful self-exertion, and serviceable citizenship.

And now that a settled business was opening out before him at Tottenham, he turned his thoughts towards marriage.  But feeling the intense importance of serious consideration, before permanently and irrevocably uniting himself to one whose influence on his present and eternal welfare must, necessarily, very materially decide the good or the evil of his existence, he again had recourse to reverent fervent prayer, and entreated some intimation or confirmation from the Lord.  He writes, "I besought the Lord to guide me by his counsel, in taking this very momentous step; and I thought I had good ground to believe He was pleased to grant my request, and pointed out to me one who was to be my companion for life, Mary Pace, a virtuous woman of honest parents, to whom, in due time, I made proposals of marriage; and, in 1778, we were united in the solemn covenant of marriage."

The young couple commenced housekeeping in a very quiet and thrifty style, keeping no servant, and diligently seeking to set an honest and industrious example.  Success followed their endeavours; and, after twenty-seven years thus spent in the shoe-trade at Tottenham, Thomas had accumulated property which brought him in an income of about a hundred pounds a year.  He believed it his duty to be content with this, and to retire upon it from further active operations in trade, in order that he might devote himself uninterruptedly to the Lord's service, and to the benefit of his fellow-creatures.  He had already felt called upon to express frequently, amongst the Friends and others, words of religious counsel and exhortation.  He had taken several preaching journeys into the counties around the Metropolis, and had become recognized as a useful and faithful minister of the Gospel, although still, after the manner of the Friends, actively and industriously prosecuting his trade. But at length, in 1805, at the age of fifty-one, he thus states his inward impression and conviction :—" An apprehension was at times presented to my mind that the time was fast approaching when I must be willing to relinquish a good business which I had been helped to get together, and set myself more at liberty to attend to my religious duties from home, by the language which my Divine Master renewedly proclaimed in the ear of my soul, of ' Gather up thy wares into thine house, for I have need of the residue of thy days ' ; accompanied by an assurance, that although there was, as some would consider, but little meal in the barrel, and little oil in the cruse, of temporal property (not having realized more than a bare hundred pounds a year, and all my five children to settle in the world), if I was but faithful in giving up to this and every future requiring of my great Creator, the meal and oil should not waste.

" I endeavoured to weigh this requisition of my Divine Master in the best way my feeble capacity was equal to, and well knew that the meal and oil He had thus condescended to give in store, would be amply sufficient for me and my dear wife, should we be permitted to see old age, provided we continued to pursue our economical habits, and that I must leave the provision for my children's settling in life to that same Almighty Power who had so abundantly cared for us; yet the prospect of relinquishing a good business, as my son declined taking to it, was at times a close trial of my faith. The requiring, however, pressed upon me with increasing weight, accompanied with a fear that if I did not endeavour, after a cheerful resignation of myself and my all (which a kind Providence had given us for our declining years) to his disposal, even all this would be blasted again, without power on my part, with my utmost caution and care to prevent."

Knowing that even solemn impressions of duty, on matters not clearly laid down in Holy Scripture, might sometimes be misapprehensions, Thomes Shillitoe wisely took counsel with some of his most experienced religious acquaintances. These, after a full consideration of the subject, approved his faith, and advised compliance.

A suitable opportunity soon occurred for disposing of his business, and thenceforth, Thomas Shillitoe, untrammelled by secular cares, devoted himself to the home and foreign service of his Lord and of the churches. He considered it an indication of the Divine pleasure at the sacrifice that he had now made, that, shortly after his retirement from trade, on the decease of a person from whom he had not the slightest expectation, it was found that in her will she had bequeathed Mr. Shillitoe a hundred pounds. This was an acceptable and seasonable gift, which he gratefully ascribed to the interposition of his Heavenly Father.

In 1806, about a year after Thomas Shillitoe had, as he supposed, wound up his affairs, it was further impressed upon his mind that he would not be completely disentangled from secular cares, until he had also freed himself from the obligations connected with some leasehold property held by sub-tenants under him. As this prospect threatened to reduce his income more than ever, he was not in a hurry to act upon it, and took two years to turn it over in his mind. But at length, in 1808, having made all needful arrangements for a preaching journey in Ireland, Thomas Shillitoe found his mind so "clouded" with a sense of the absence of the Lord's comforting presence, compared with other times, that he was brought into very close self-examination as to the cause, and it then appeared clear to him that his retention of the lease-holds was the source of his difficulty. He then arranged finally, both with his landlord and with the tenants, to free himself from the leasehold covenants; and, owing to the liberality of the former, the terms agreed upon were such as rendered Thomas Shillitoe's income henceforth greater, instead of less, than before. Thus, again, his faithfulness was rewarded; and, in addition, he found himself completely disentangled from obligations which had, at times, engrossed much of his attention, and which might have led to perplexities unfavourable to a life devoted to Christian ministry.

Although, amongst the Friends, some of the ministers leave their outward occupations at times, to undertake Gospel journeys, yet the greater number of their actively engaged preachers are such as have retired from business, or have been placed in comfortable circumstances, sufficient at least to remove them from temporal anxieties whilst ministering. Thomas Shillitoe now became one of this number, and henceforth his Gospel labours increased manifold.

# CHAPTER III.

## HIS HOME MISSIONS AND ORDINARY MINISTRY.

HABITUAL PEDESTRIAN MINISTRY—EXTRAORDINARY SPELLS OF WALKING—AN EXCESSIVELY HOT DAY—FREE AND EASY STYLE OF DRESS—LOVE OF LABOUR, BOTH SPIRITUAL AND MANUAL—HIS INTEMPERATE FOREMAN, AND THE REWARD OF FAITHFULNESS—PRAYERFUL TRUST IN GOD—SENSE OF DEPENDENCE THE MEASURE OF CHRISTIAN PROGRESS—FAITH DEVELOPED BY EFFORT—INDISPENSABLE NECESSITY FOR THE VISITATIONS OF THE HOLY SPIRIT—"LAYING ON HARD"—ILLUSTRATION OF MR. SHILLITOE'S STYLE OF RELIGIOUS ADDRESS—EFFORTS AMONGST THE KINGSWOOD COLLIERS—PROVISION FOR SUFFERERS BY COLLIERY ACCIDENTS—"COMPEL THEM TO COME IN"—VISITS TO THE WIDOWS AND ORPHANS OF EXECUTED MACHINE-BREAKERS—ZEALOUS ATTENTION EVEN TO EFFORTS FOR SINGLE INDIVIDUALS.

THOMAS SHILLITOE had commenced his ministry by occasional exhortations in the meetings of the Friends very soon after his union with their Society, at about the age of twenty-five. During the following twenty-five years he continued to preach occasionally, and several times undertook short journeys on his religious errands. But until his retirement from business in 1805 (at the age of fifty-one), he had not entered extensively on the sphere of labour which henceforth characterized him. With the exception of a brief visit to the Channel Islands, Calais, and Dunkirk, his travels previous to this period do not

appear to have extended further than Lincolnshire, or to
have occupied, in the aggregate, more than about ten
months during the twenty-five years. But, after his retirement from business, his home and foreign religious
labours were abundant and continuous. Faithfully, and
with humble entireness of dedication, he surrendered
"the residue of his days" to the arduous exercises of
ministerial travel.

Mr. Ruskin has somewhere remarked that, in the days
of our Lord and his Apostles, the Gospel was promulgated
only "at a walking pace." And, on recurring to the New
Testament, it is certainly noticeable that, notwithstanding
the comparatively high civilization of Palestine in the time
of our Saviour, the earliest promulgators of Christianity
were habitually pedestrians in their labours of love. The
Evangelists repeatedly allude to the journeys on foot of
that sacred band, foremost amongst whom was their
Divine Lord and Leader. And when, on other occasions,
they went forth two and two, they received the command
"that they should take nothing for their journey save a
staff only," inasmuch as those who received the blessing
of their services were to supply all needful wants; and
when this return was not accorded, the further command
was "Shake off the dust under your feet for a testimony
against them." In the Acts of the Apostles also, there
are allusions to the general pedestrian movements of the
Apostles. Of Philip, for instance, it is recorded that he
"ran" towards the Ethiopian noble, who, riding homeward in his chariot, was reading the pages of Isaiah.
Other modes of travel were, doubtless, always permissible
and often preferable. Nevertheless, for various reasons,

the Apostolic missionaries appear to have usually chosen the independence and freedom of walking. Thus of Paul we read that when he had the option of proceeding from Troas to Assos by ship with his companions, or on land without them, he chose the latter course, "minding himself to go afoot" (Acts xx. 13). Probably the quiet opportunity thus afforded for meditation and secret prayer was the deciding motive in the latter instance.

Partly for a similar reason, partly on economical grounds, and also probably from a love of independent and free movement, Thomas Shillitoe very often performed his preaching journeys on foot. He was characteristically a pedestrian religious itinerant. His memoranda abound in such records as the following :—"After meeting I walked to Castleton, ten miles ; had a comfortable meeting with a few Friends there next morning. In the afternoon walked to Whitby, fourteen miles over a dreary moor. After it I walked to Russell Dale, and next day to Helmsley ; in the afternoon to Bilsdale. Next day walked about thirty-two miles to Knaresborough, and next day to Rawden. I walked to Lothersdale, about twenty-two miles. The great quantity of rain that has fallen of late has made travelling on foot trying : I hope to be preserved in the patience, apprehending it is the line of conduct I must pursue when time will allow of it. Next day walked to Netherdale, about twenty-four miles."

The continuity of Thomas Shillitoe's pedestrianism was sometimes extraordinary. Thus, in one week he mentions walking on a Saturday evening from Lancaster to Wyersdale ; on the Sunday afternoon to Ray ; on the Monday twenty-six miles to Hawes ; on Tuesday twenty-eight

miles to Masham; on Wednesday twenty-three miles to
Leyburn; on Thursday eight miles to Aysgarth, and the
same afternoon ten miles over the moor to Reeth. On
Friday he set out with a horse and chaise to return to
Hawes, but finding the dales were at that time flooded in
many places owing to the recent heavy rains, he quitted
the conveyance and recommenced walking, often coming
to places where the usual crossing by stepping-stones was
impracticable, and where he had to wade through the
rushing streams. However, he reached Hawes safely,
and, fortified by a good dinner, boldly struck over the
fells to Brigflatts, whence on Saturday he walked to
Kendal, and reached Lancaster in the evening. Such
was a week's work of this zealous and simple-hearted
evangelist!

Repeatedly he proceeded on foot by rapid stages across
England at a similar pace to the Yorkshire journey just
described. Thus in the same year (1807) he walked from
Liverpool to Warrington, thence to Macclesfield, on a
Saturday, a journey of twenty-three miles. On the
Sabbath morning he walked thirteen miles to Leek, and
held a meeting there. He started again on foot on
Monday, and performed twenty-nine miles to Derby;
then the next day another thirty miles to Leicester; on
Wednesday walked twenty-nine miles to Northampton.
"The day proving wet, travelling became more difficult;
but now, drawing so near home operated as a spur to do
my best." On Thursday he accomplished twenty-three
miles to Woburn, and on Friday walked the remaining
*thirty-nine* miles, which brought him safe back to his
family.

One reason for his preference of walking is indicated in a memorandum in which he writes : " Proceeded by boat to Warrington (from Manchester) with a mixed company, whereby I found myself deprived of that quiet opportunity for reflection, which my usual mode of travelling affords me ; leaving the boat, I walked to Liverpool."

Thomas Shillitoe found the inconveniences of summer heat often greater than those of winter rains. In the extraordinary season of the year 1809, in July, he was again walking across England, on his way to Ireland. Having arrived at the village of Lower Heaford, after a walk of thirty miles thither the preceding day, he started thence towards Hinckley, in Leicestershire. As the district was very thinly populated, and the roads not frequented by many travellers, it was not likely that he would be able to meet with any entertainment, except perhaps at one place. Accordingly, his host at Heaford supplied him with a bottle of cider and some bread as an equipment for the day's needs. With this not very luxurious provision the good man started on his way, but as early as nine o'clock was almost brought to a stand by the unprecedented heat. He writes, " I was overcome by it, and obliged to have such frequent recourse to my cider and bread, it was soon exhausted. I made but little progress in getting forward, although, by stripping off most of my apparel, I relieved myself all in my power. By twelve o'clock the air became so affected in the shade, I felt as if I was surrounded every way by heat from a fire. As yet I had not passed an habitation of any de-scription, nor met or seen man, woman, child, or any living animal." After the long drought and heat, the pools and ditches contained no water. But Mr. Shillitoe perceiving a bridge at a distance, eagerly turned his steps towards it, hoping to find a stream where he might quench his intense thirst. There was indeed a little stagnant water remaining, and in the midst of this a cow was stamping her feet for a little coolness. Almost ready to perish, Mr. Shillitoe drank of the nauseous liquid, and filled his bottle with some for the remainder of his journey. Stripping off most of his clothes, he carried them in a bundle on his back, and again crept wearily along. By and by he met a boy whom he paid to carry his bundle to the nearest house, a mile distant. There he offered a seven-shilling piece to be conveyed one mile further to a wayside inn. But before starting he was so exhausted that it was necessary for him to lie down awhile on a bed. When somewhat recruited, he resumed his way on a pony. But so excessive was the heat that, he records, "The gooseberries on the trees next morning appeared, where they were exposed to the sun, as if they had been in an oven or saucepan on the fire. Near fifty horses, it was reported, had dropped down dead on the north road, and many people who were working in the fields. It was supposed to have been the hottest day known in this nation."

Thomas Shillitoe sometimes carried his love of independence and simplicity to an excess, both when on his itinerant missions and on other occasions. From being the smart gentlemanly banker's clerk, he had become so careless of his outward appearance, as to be often barely respectable in aspect. Clad in a "pepper and salt" suit, with dowlais shirt, often open at the neck, without cravat, and with a chip hat in hot weather carried in his hand, or deposited on the top of his umbrella, whilst he paced vigorously along with his coat on his arm, he sometimes caused a sensation of amusement and surprise in those who met him.  On one occasion, Mrs. Shillitoe being apprehensive that her husband would over-exert himself by his long walking, gave private instructions to a coachman to stop his vehicle on a certain road, along which Thomas had started, and to importune the latter to mount the stage.  On the coachman enquiring, " But how shall I know your husband from any other man, madam? " She replied that if he met a man unlike any other man, " that's my husband."  Guided by this description, the driver recognized Mr. Shillitoe on overtaking him, and conveyed to him the request of his good wife, with which he forthwith obediently complied.

We have heard it related of him that during one of his religious visits to Yorkshire, some wealthy friends, not personally acquainted with him, were expecting Thomas to take up his lodging at their house, during a certain gathering of their brethren.  When Thomas came to the house, in his usual unceremonious style and appearance, he was presumed to be some poor rustic Friend from the district, and was forthwith invited into the kitchen, where the servants were to bring him some refreshment.  He, perceiving his non-recognition, quietly went thither as requested, and afterwards at meeting his hosts were much surprised to find that the chief preacher on the occasion was their unknown kitchen friend, the expected Thomas Shillitoe.  It may be presumed he took his next meal in the dining-room.

When very far advanced in life, Thomas one day came

into town from Tottenham, to join a deputation of Friends appointed to present an address to King William the Fourth, on his accession to the throne. As usual, Thomas had his coat off, but was not aware of a conspicuous hole in his shirt. One of the deputation promptly drew his attention to the condition of his under garment, and for that time, at least, Thomas proceeded with his coat on like other folks.

His dislike of inactivity was extreme. When, on his journeys, he was obliged to intermit his preaching, he endeavoured to fill up the intervals by useful occupation. He sometimes carried with him a linen smock-frock, similar to that worn by agricultural labourers, to wear whilst engaged in manual employment at farm-houses where he might be staying. After a hard day's work at the unaccustomed employment of cutting oats, he mentions, "feeling very stiff, and being truly glad when night came," but adds that he believed it his duty to set an example of industry to the people and their preachers.

He was as simple in his diet as in other matters. The last fifty years of his life he was both a teetotaler and a vegetarian, except as to the use of milk and eggs. The latter he was very fond of, and ate them raw. When on his pedestrian missions he would, at times, take his dinner by calling in at a cottage or way-side shop, where he would obtain some bread and a few eggs. It often excited amusement in the spectators when they saw him thus suck egg after egg uncooked.

A recently deceased friend of Mr. Shillitoe mentioned that on one occasion the latter arrived late at night at his house, at Northampton, and, on being asked what he

would like for supper, replied that he would prefer a bason
of warm water and treacle. After being supplied with
this, he retired to bed. Early next morning he started
off before breakfast, and walked on another stage to his
morning meal.

The first time Thomas Shillitoe left home on a religious
mission, was to go into Norfolk. Before starting he felt
very uneasy at the prospect of leaving his business under
the care of his foreman, who, although a clever workman,
was apt at times to give much trouble by his intemperance,
and hence had little authority over the other men, even in
his master's presence. Therefore, in the absence of the
latter, things might be expected to be worse. At this
period also (1791) robberies and burglaries were frequent
at Tottenham and elsewhere, and Mr. Shillitoe feared
leaving his wife and young family under the careless oversight of the foreman. Whilst one day pondering these
difficulties, when in his shop cutting out work for the men,
there came upon him a clear and impressive conviction of
his duty, to go forth on his Gospel errand, trusting on
the protection of his Lord.

He states that this impression was communicated to
him " in a language as intelligible as ever I heard words
spoken to my outward ear," and declaring, as from the
Lord, " I will be more than bolts and bars to thy outward
habitation; more than a master to my servants, for I can
restrain their wandering minds; more than a husband to
thy wife, and a parent to thy infant children." Thomas
adds that, on receiving this impression, " the knife I was
using fell out of my hand, I no longer daring to hesitate
after such a confirmation." Forthwith in faith and

gratitude he left home, and spent between two and three months in the accomplishment of his mission. On his return to Tottenham he found his family well, and his business affairs in as satisfactory a condition as if his personal oversight had not been withdrawn; and he received from his friends assurances of the remarkable industry and sobriety of the foreman in his absence. A few days after Mr. Shillitoe's return, the latter relapsed into his former habits, and rambled off from his situation. Thomas adds, "After such evident demonstrations of the all-sufficiency of the superintending care of the Most High, what must I expect will be the sad consequences of unfaithfulness to Divine requirings, should it in a future day mark my footsteps!"

It was a characteristic of Mr. Shillitoe, as it is of many of his brother Friends, to entertain a reverential and faithful trust in the reality of God's superintending providence. He believed that, although men are governed by fixed laws, and although in general the Christian walks by faith and "*not* by sight" (or by such indubitable evidence as could be equivalent in clearness to outward sight), yet that all human actions and events are under the Divine control and observation. He also believed that, in order to ascertain the Lord's will concerning him, it was essential (as it certainly is to every Christian) to cherish daily habits of humble effort and fervent prayer, in addition to the reverent perusal of "the great things of God's law" in Holy Scripture.

This was indeed one of the most characteristic traits of Thomas Shillitoe's life—his unremitting prayerfulness for Divine guidance and light. Whether engaged in home missions, or in foreign travel, he desired day by day to commit his way to the Lord, that He might bring it to pass.

And it was equally characteristic of his preaching, that he always set forth the special and abiding necessity of a conviction of the entire weakness of man as man, and of a spirit of complete dependence upon God. It has been justly remarked by a thoughtful writer that, inasmuch as all men are alike sinful by nature, and possess no differences of virtue or superiority, except such as are the free gifts of God's sovereign goodness, and are entirely independent of any deserving qualities in the recipients, so the chief feature wherein Christians differ from unconverted men, or from each other, consists in their respective attainments in realizing their own absolute emptiness of good, and the perpetual indispensableness of consulting the laws of God in the Bible, and of prayer for the aid of His Spirit purchased by the death and resurrection of our Lord Jesus Christ. In other words, the Christian's growth in grace is his growth in childlike dependence upon the Lord. Like the ivy, "the strength it gains is from the embrace it gives." All fruitfulness in the religious life must spring from an increased taking root *downwards* in prayerful recourse to God, and an increasing experience of human unreliableness. This is always acknowledged by truly good men. They feel increasingly, as they grow in grace, the truth of the apostolic appeal, "What hast thou that thou didst not receive?" And when they behold around them the wickedness and ungodliness of those whose absence of educational and religious blessings is the sufficient explanation of their unfortunate condition, they are ready to exclaim as good John Bradford did when he saw a criminal being led to execution—"There, but for the grace of God, goes myself." Further, the really experienced Christian feels that past efforts will not sustain him in the future. He has absolutely *nothing* in himself that will remain strong for good, apart from a continued and ever-renewed recourse to God by prayer, by effort, and by the enkindling meditation on his statute law of the Scriptures. As the manna gathered by the Israelites was valueless for the morrow, as the meal of one day does not suffice for the next, so also, in God's appointment, each day must witness its own distinct search for the bread of life by prayer, and by the seeking of the Holy Spirit's aid, especially through His chosen and most honoured channel the thoughtful and humble use of His own written oracles.

This great doctrine that the degree of a Christian's heartfelt prayerful dependence on his Lord, is also the precise measure of his religious growth, constituted, under various forms, a frequent subject of Thomas Shillitoe's preaching, both at home and abroad.

Another characteristic of his ministry was the prominence he attached to practical religious effort. Like the Apostle James, he repeatedly urged that "faith without works is dead." Like James, too, he taught that not only must works spring from faith, but that also, by a striking exemplification of the universal law of mutual reaction, works increase faith. Thus it was with Abraham, "Seest thou not how faith wrought with his works, and *by works was faith made perfect.*" So, Thomas Shillitoe constantly impressed upon his hearers that it was in vain for them to call themselves Christians, unless they strove to obey the

laws of their invisible but really living Lord Jesus; and
that if they put forth diligent efforts to act out His precepts
of charity and zeal, they would, in precisely the same
measure, have their sense of the actuality of Christ's
existence increased.    Further, the more they strove to
obey His commands, the more they would feel their own
weakness; hence, the more they would be constrained to
pray, and then, through prayer, they would receive more
faith which, like every other good thing, is "the gift of
God." So, continuing faithful and striving to the end,
they would finally receive at Christ's appearing the
crowning boon of all, "the gift of eternal life" by the
power of Christ, who has promised to every believer in
Himself, "I will raise him up at the last day."

One other frequent subject of his preaching was the
preciousness and indispensability of the visitations of God's
Holy Spirit to the heart of man, by which we feel Him to
be a *living* God, and a real hearer and answerer of prayer.
We are not to expect any new revelation of His *Law;* for
this is *already given* in the Holy Scriptures, "that the
man of God may be perfect, *thoroughly* furnished unto all
good works." Nevertheless, these sacred laws are not
effectually realized and received with practical power into
the heart, except by the further gift of the energizing
influences of the Divine constraints and restraints often
manifested to the soul.    This was, throughout his life,
clearly enforced by Thomas Shillitoe.    His doctrine
respecting it, which is that of earnest Christians in
general, may be succinctly given in the words of a pious
clergyman of the Church of England, viz.:—

"The supposition that the habits and virtues of religion

may be acquired by our own unaided efforts, proceeds on an entirely mistaken view of the subject. For *what* are the habits and virtues to be acquired? They are supreme love to God; an entire subjection to His will; a lively faith in the Redeemer's death as an atonement for sin; a profound and unfeigned humility; a renunciation of self, both righteous and sinful; and a complete mastery over everything prohibited by the Divine precepts.

"But our own experience, the moral history of mankind, as well as the confessions and prayers of good and great men in all ages, prove that the acquirement of these are painful and laborious; and if painful and laborious they are not natural, and if not natural it seems impossible to escape from the conclusion that Divine assistance is necessary." ("On the Nature of Divine Agency," by the Rev. Stephen Davies. London: Hatchard & Co. 1836.)

Thomas Shillitoe preached boldly and decidedly. His voice was very loud, and often made the walls echo. A favourite phrase with him was, "Persuaded I am;" and this was delivered with an emphatic and positive laying down of his convictions which commanded attention. He was especially stern in his denunciations of extravagance and carelessness in professing Christians. On a certain occasion, after one of his authoritative rebukes to a congregation in which were many wealthy Friends, one of them afterwards complained to him that he had "laid on hard." Thomas received the hint in a pleasant manner, and carefully reconsidered his address and the reasons for it, but adds that he felt satisfied and confirmed that it had been right. He remembered the words addressed on a

similar occasion to another bold preacher by a fellow
Quaker, an elder, who said, " Young man, 'tis soft knocks
must enter hard blocks." "True, sometimes," was the
response; "but when a tree is rotten at the heart it
requires a few smart strokes to cause the wedge to enter,
otherwise it rebounds again."

Thomas Shillitoe not unfrequently administered " smart
strokes," especially to the wealthy and indifferent; but he
was also truly " a son of consolation" to the afflicted and
the poor.   As a sample of his bold and vigorous style, we
may quote the following from an address issued by him to
the Society of Friends :—

" How many among us are pursuing their worldly
concerns as if they counted gain godliness, and not, as
must be the case with the true disciples and followers of
Christ, godliness, with contentment, to be the greatest
riches (1 Tim. vi. 5, 6); proclaiming in the language of
conduct, that all is fish that comes to their net, regarding
neither quantity nor quality, so there be a prospect of a
good profit attached to it.   Oh! these professing world-
lings, who say they are Jews, and are not, but whose
fruits testify they are of the synagogue of Satan, I have
been persuaded have been the greatest enemies to the
spreading of our religious principles, and the enlargement
of our borders; those who maintain a uniform consistent
warfare against the Babylonish garment (Joshua vi. 21),
but, with all their might, grasp at the wedge of gold, and
aim at making a splendid appearance in their way of
living."

" We may be active in Society concerns, and yet
strangers to this religious exercise, without which we

cannot become helpers in the Lord's cause, and lights in the world.''

" It is my belief the day of the Lord is coming upon every one that is proud and lofty, and upon every one that is ' lifted up, and he shall be brought low ; and upon all the cedars of Lebanon that are high and lifted up, and upon all the oaks of Bashan, and upon all the high moun- tains, and upon all the hills that are lifted, and upon every high tower, and upon every fenced wall, and upon all the ships of Tarshish, and upon all pleasant pictures.' (Isaiah ii. 12-16.)

" You must be willing, mothers and children, to examine closely the mode and circumstances of your ex- penditure, with a mind made up to.relieve, as far as in you lies, the head of the family, who may have both wind and tide to contend with. Search your houses, search your tables, search your garments ; and, where any ex- pense can be spared without lessening your real comforts, seek for holy help to rid the vessel of it. I am well aware it will require holy help to take such steps. Regard not the world's dread laugh.

" And, Friends, you that are of ability of body, learn to wait more upon yourselves, and bring your children to do the like. I find I am never better waited on than when I wait upon myself. Teach your children industry and a well-regulated economy ; for, next to a truly pious example, you cannot bestow upon your children a better portion. Suitable employment, under the influence of an all-wise Creator, is salutary both for mind and body, and qualifies us the better to feel for, and proportion labour to,

those who may be placed under us. And where this
well-regulated industry and economy are wanting, and
idleness and fulness of bread prevail, how little is to be
observed in the conduct of such, of reverential thankfulness for the bounties they are receiving from
heaven.

" When we are content to move in this humble sphere,
we are prepared the better to meet such reverses as may
come upon us. Let none among us say in his heart I am
out of the reach of reverses, because none are out of the
reach of them ; for, however variously our outward sub-
stance may be secured, *all sublunary things are unstable as
the waters.*"

Thomas Shillitoe's ministry abundantly illustrated that
characteristic of Christianity, "to the poor the Gospel is
preached." Very much of his religious effort was directed
towards this class. Thus, in the autumn of 1812, having
been informed of the squalid and neglected condition of
the Kingswood colliers, near Bristol, he left his comfortable home, and spent several weeks in arduous, persevering visitation of these poor creatures from cottage to
cottage. He directed special attention to a numerous
band of thieves and housebreakers amongst them, who
went by the name of "the gang," and whose ranks for
many years supplied the prisons and the gallows of Glou-
cestershire with a constant supply of criminal subjects.
His heart felt tenderly for the many widows and orphans
in this district, whose husbands and fathers had lost their
lives in their dangerous labours. "Killed in the pit,
sir," "killed in the pit, sir," was the repeated reply to

his enquiries as to what had become of the head of the family in many of the cottages he visited.*

During the visits of Mr. Shillitoe and his companion to the colliers, the latter, although their black and grimy faces gave them a repulsive look, evinced much serious-

---

* COLLIERY ACCIDENTS.—Of late years the British public has been, from time to time, appalled by the enormous loss of life consequent upon colliery explosions. Thus, at the catastrophe at the Hartley Pit, near Newcastle, "upwards of two hundred bodies were brought to the surface, and distributed amongst the widows and mothers of the pitman's village." Double as many deaths occurred at the terrific explosion at the Oaks Colliery, near Barnsley, in December, 1866. On these and other occasions the national sympathies were roused to noble efforts for the bereaved survivors. But in many other instances, where the loss of life has been less noticeable, there has been no special provision made for the sufferers. In a letter recently addressed to a public journal by Mr. W. M. Wilkinson, of Lincoln's-inn Fields, it is stated that in the ten years years ending 1860, 9090 lives of miners were lost in the collieries. During those ten years 605,154,940 tons of coal were raised, so that one person was killed for each 66,573 tons of coal raised from the pits. Since 1860 the loss of life in this manner appears to have increased. It may fairly be assumed that at least one thousand lives are annually sacrificed in obtaining the coal for our comfortable firesides and gas-lamps.

Mr. Wilkinson suggests the levying of a slight tax upon every colliery to form a permanently available fund for the relief of the families whose supporters perish in the works. Taking one life for every 66,573 tons of coal as the statistical basis for calculating the requisite fund to be raised, Mr. Wilkinson estimates that the average imposition on each colliery would be about £15 per pit. An officer to be appointed by the Board of Trade might manage the collection and distribution. Such a system would, it is believed, tend to render owners and workmen more careful and vigilant, and would provide timely relief for the survivors of persons sacrificed in the ordinary and comparatively unnoticed accidents of every year, as well as for the specially sensational occurrences.

ness, and respectfully received the sympathizing counsels extended to them. The energy displayed by the good Friends in looking up the objects of their interest was most persevering. Thus, in passing over a common on his way to some cottages, Mr. Shillitoe espied two men catching birds, a favourite pastime with "the gang;" but the latter, seeing a stranger coming after them, speedily made off, as if afraid of apprehension. Thomas put on speed, too, and presently overtook the elder of the couple, who, being an old man, was unable to climb over a high gate in his way with sufficient quickness to escape. He was now kindly invited to step into a cottage, and listen to the address of the good Friends. His companion also must be brought in if possible. The latter had been seen to enter a house which had no back door, and from which it was therefore certain he could not have again left without observation. But on Thomas making enquiry there, a woman boldly denied that any man had entered. On being again urged to call him, and seriously warned against the sin of falsehood, she at length called out several times, "Richard, come down stairs!" but no response being given, Mr. Shillitoe also called out, adding that he must come up and fetch Richard down, if the latter did not make his appearance. At length Thomas went boldly upstairs, and found "a large-boned hale young man" crouching down behind the head of a bed. Thomas would have been nothing in his hands had the gangsman been permitted to assault him. But the worthy Friend took him by the collar, told him he wanted his company down-stairs, and sent him on before him to the chimney corner, where he quietly seated himself, and listened attentively

to the exhortations of his bold visitor, of whom, on parting, he took leave in a kind and grateful manner, affording some ground for hope that real good had been effected
in the case. In his instance, as with very many others of
"the gang," he had been early trained to crime by his
father.

Another work of love which, in the year 1813, claimed
Thomas Shillitoe's Christian zeal, was a series of visits to
the widows and orphans of seventeen men who had just
been hanged at York for conspiracy and riotous violence
against the users of machinery in the neighbourhood of
Huddersfield. These misguided men, not having learnt
that machinery tends to increase labour in a greater
degree eventually than its immediate diminution, had
gone the length of murdering one of the manufacturers
in addition to a wholesale destruction of property.

A wide-spread feeling of terror and insecurity ensued,
and to restore order it was deemed necessary to inflict the
extreme penalty of the law on the miserable offenders.
In the course of the visits to the sorrowing relatives of
these, Mr. Shillitoe's sympathies were profoundly moved
by the heartrending narratives of grief and desolation
which, from house to house, he had to listen to. Thus
the wife of a young man who had been dragged into the
conspiracy, and whose execution had left her a widow
with a helpless infant to provide for, stated that the night
her husband was arrested, he had been forced out of bed
by the gang, who had hurried him away with them to the
work of destruction. The terrified young woman, half
clad, ran a long distance after her husband, imploring him
to return; but his infuriated companions drove her back,

E

threatening to blow her brains out if she persisted in her entreaties. Before his untimely death he became penitent, and died in humble contrition for his sins, and with a heartfelt hope of experiencing the mercy of Christ hereafter. And, doubtless, such hopes were not to be disappointed. For our Lord Jesus Christ, "the image of the invisible God," pre-eminently set forth to men His great attributes of justice and mercy. In dealing with poor erring creatures, "born in sin and shapen in iniquity," mercy becomes an inseparable element of true justice. The merits of the glorious Cross of Jesus flow broadly over the multitude of penitent and suppliant ones who, like the serpent-bitten Israelites in their wilderness misery, look with yearning eyes towards the infinite love of the Holy One, who, in view of His own voluntary and Divine sacrifice, exclaimed, "I, if I be lifted up, will draw all men unto Me." And in the coming ages of His Kingdom, it will, we may rest confidently assured, be manifested that the sacred light and life radiating, thenceforth for ever, from His "great white throne" will include within their influences many who, like the dying thief on Calvary, have even at the eleventh hour, in heartfelt repentance and fervent prayer stretched forth suppliant hands towards the free gift of mercy purchased by the sufferings and love of Christ the Redeemer.

As another illustration of the zeal and industry which characterized Thomas Shillitoe's labours for the good of individuals, as well as of groups and communities, the following case may be mentioned. He had felt much regret at the obstinacy of a person who, in a distant part of England, persisted in cherishing a spirit of bitterness in connection with a private quarrel which ought long previously to have been terminated. Mr. Shillitoe was about to start for a long continental journey, but could not comfortably quit England until he had made an effort towards effecting the reconciliation of this individual with the parties from whom he kept himself estranged. He therefore left home in quest of the delinquent. On quitting the stage he had thirty miles to walk. It was a cold winter day, and deep snow covered the ground; but Mr. Shillitoe persevered in his pursuit until he reached his destination, where, to his extreme disappointment, he ascertained that the object of his search had a few days previously quitted his residence for a place sixty miles off. But thither Thomas determined to follow him, and, after three days' additional travel, succeeded in obtaining an interview, and urging his friendly counsels of peace. It does not appear whether or not this Christian endeavour was wholly successful; but, at any rate, it was courteously received, and afforded hearty satisfaction to the good man who, at so much cost of personal ease and of valuable time, exerted himself in its performance.

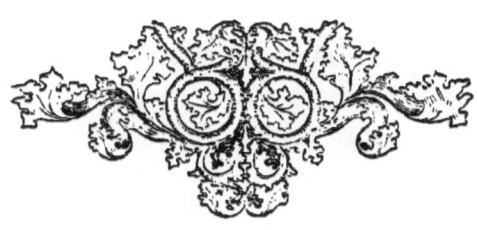

# CHAPTER IV.

## HIS FOREIGN MISSIONS.

SERIOUS PROSPECT OF EXTENSIVE TRAVEL AT HIS ADVANCED
AGE—THE PROVINCE OF REASON—THE HICKSITES—BREAKS
UP HIS HOME—FIVE CHIEF OBJECTS OF EFFORT—DAILY
BREATHING-TIMES OF THE SPIRITUAL LIFE—ECONOMY OF
EFFORT — HIS CHEERFULNESS AND PLEASANTNESS — HIS
GALLANTRY — LOCKED UP AT ALTONA — HONOURED AT
HAMBURG—MISHAPS OF DANISH TRAVEL—SUCCESS AT
COPENHAGEN—A BLACK GUIDE—NEW YEAR'S FESTIVITIES
IN NORWAY — MAGNIFICENT SCENERY — PRUSSIA AND
GERMANY—A FRIENDS' MEETING CONDUCTED UNDER DIFFI-
CULTIES—DUMB ELOQUENCE—HOME THROUGH SWITZERLAND
AND FRANCE.

AFTER many years of arduous Christian effort in Great
Britain and Ireland, Thomas Shillitoe, in 1821, at the
advanced age of sixty-seven, undertook a series of extensive
missionary efforts on the continent of Europe; and, at a
still later period, crossed the Atlantic to labour in America
also.

It was a very serious prospect indeed to the venerable
minister of Christ so to devote himself, and at that period
of life, to such an enterprise.   He thus speaks of his contemplation of the duty :—" When I am led to take a view
of the accumulated difficulties that I must expect in the
prosecution of the work before me, my soul is humbled
and bowed within me as into the very dust; whereby my

mind at times became sorrowfully charged with an apprehension I should not have strength to proceed agreeably
to the expectation I had given my friends, and thereby
shamefully expose myself. But Divine Goodness appeared
for my help with this animating assurance, that if I re-
mained willing to become *like a cork on the mighty ocean*
of service which my great Master should require of me, in
the storm and in the calm, free from the lead of human
reason, not consulting and conferring with flesh and blood,
willing to be wafted hither and thither as the Spirit of the
Lord my God should blow upon me, He would care for
me every day and every way; so that there should be no
lack of strength to encounter all my difficulties. Here
my discouragements vanished."

In this beautiful and touching acknowledgment of entire
dedication to his Lord, and of child-like absolute trust
upon His guidance, there is one indication of a conclusion
which will not bear the test of experience and scriptural
examination, viz., the requirement to be " free from the
lead of human reason."

Reason is one of God's most precious gifts to man. It
is, confessedly, insufficient, apart from revelation and
spiritual influences, to guide into salvation, as the history
of the most enlightened nations of antiquity abundantly
proves. But, *so far as its province extends*, it is precious
and indispensable. Without it we should be mere machines,
moved as by mechanical impulse, and incapable of receiving
moral or religious development, as in the case of idiots.
Without it there would be no meaning in the command of
Christ, " Search the Scriptures, for in them ye think ye
have eternal life, and they are they which testify of Me."

Without it even religious impulses would be dishonoured
to the level of mere instinctive motions such as those
which impel the beaver in the construction of its dam, or
the swallow in the season of its migration.  Without it,
moral freedom and intelligent loving choice of God and
of Christ would be impossible.  Without it, man would
abide in a state of everlasting infancy,—innocent perhaps,
but by no means righteous, or loving, or grateful, or
humble, or patient, or faithful, or just,—for all these
qualities require the exercise and the conclusions of reason
and of experimental reflection.

Reason has pre-eminently its use in the religious life.
The author of the work on "Divine Agency," already
quoted, aptly remarks,—"The office of reason clearly is,
to examine the *claims* of the Scriptures to inspiration; to
ascertain by every possible means the *genuine sense* of their
contents; and then to bow implicitly to their *authority* as
to that from which there lies no appeal."

It might be added, that although reason helps us to
examine and to understand the precepts of Revelation, she
can never create revelation, nor is she sufficient to furnish
us with the dispositions and the spiritual forces sufficient
to enable us to act upon even her own directions.  The
most talented men, aided by reason, but not having the
further gifts of Christ and of His Holy Spirit, have had
oftentimes to confess with helpless humiliation that they

> " See the right, and yet the wrong pursue."

And so it ever will be.  Reason is an instrument for the
use and management of the material afforded by revelation;
but it is not the material itself, neither is it even the
exclusive or sufficient instrument for the purpose.

The particular and distinctive operations for which God has endowed man with reason, can in general only be performed by it; for God honours all His own gifts. Just as we are not to expect any special revelation to inform us of the existence or nature of the objects which our outward senses are already given us to manifest, so also it is vain to expect that the Lord's Spirit will require us to neglect or ignore that precious gift of reason which He himself has in His gracious wisdom conferred on us for use, and not for disuse.

In like manner, also, it is not to be expected that the Holy Spirit will ever reveal to man, separately from the Scriptures, "the great things of His law," which He has already manifested in that sacred gift of the Bible.

Yet, good Thomas Shillitoe, on precisely the same principle which led him at times to neglect the use of reason, sometimes also expressed himself in terms which led to misconstructions, derogatory to the honour which God has placed upon His own blessed Scriptures, the chief and clearest oracles of His Spirit. Hence, when he visited America and came amongst the Hicksites, a sect of persons who had separated from the Friends through their extreme assertion of this very principle, the non-indispensability of Holy Scripture, and the sufficiency of the Spirit's guidance *apart* from them, he was troubled by the public statements of these mistaken men concerning himself. For they claimed him at first as an adherent of their own mischievous views. Indeed, at a meeting in Long Island, habitually ministered to by Elias Hicks, the founder of that body of separatists from Quakerism which still bears his name, after listening to a sermon by Thomas Shillitoe, the former arose, and, highly commending the communication of the aged English minister, added, " I appeal to this assembly if it is not the same doctrine that ye have heard these many years past." Hicks also invited Thomas to take up his abode with him.

The occurrence of this sad heresy amongst the Friends in America, was overruled for good to their English brethren, who have since proclaimed, more clearly than ever before, the preciousness of the Holy Scriptures, their authority as the *alone fixed standard* of Christian truth, and the paramount value of the atonement of our Lord Jesus Christ, which blessed sacrifice the Hicksites disparaged.

In actual life, however, even in his religious movements, Thomas Shillitoe was far too shrewd practically to act as if "free from the lead of human reason." He weighed and considered his prospects long and carefully, took frequent counsel with his friends and acquaintances, prayed earnestly for God's overruling direction, and then, whilst proceeding in his efforts, still continued his vigilance and consultation and prayer. This explanation is needful, as some of his expressions are, occasionally, from their ambiguity, open to misinterpretation.

Before starting for his extensive Continental labours in 1821, he had to make great sacrifices, which, with much simplicity and beautiful Christian faith, he thus records :— " I took leave of my dear wife, now in the seventy-fifth year of her age, the most trying parting we ever experienced. I left her under the care of one of our daughters, and then proceeded to my cottage at Highbury, near Hitchin, which must either be kept shut up during my long absence, or parted with; but duty pointed to my parting with the cottage and furniture. My cottage to me had possessed many charms. I had laboured and toiled to make it a comfortable abode for our declining years, hoping to have kept it for our residence, until we should be taken to the house appointed for all living. Nature had many strugglings to endure before it made that free-will offering called for; but, believing it would be the most effectual way to have my mind freed from worldly cares, I yielded. So does the Most High work in us, and for us, as we are willing to devote ourselves to Him; then He fails not to make the hard things easy, and sweetens the bitter cup of self-denial. The way opened for my getting quit of all, in a manner I never looked for; and, feeling thus loosened from this earthly shackle, I made the necessary preparations for my journey."

Thomas Shillitoe's foreign labours, like his home efforts, were mainly directed to five objects, viz. :—1. Personal interviews with monarchs and dignitaries, in order to impress upon their minds an increased sense of the serious responsibilities of their position. 2. The right observance of the Sabbath. 3. The promotion of temperance, and the discouragement of official facilities for drunkenness. 4. The visitation of prisoners. 5. The encouragement of conscientious individuals, and of small communities of religious persons anxious respecting their relations to the Lord and to eternity.

As several of the above classes of efforts will be noticed separately in another portion of this work, we may here confine ourselves to some of the general aspects and most striking details of Mr. Shillitoe's missionary travels.

During his visits to interesting localities, the one great purpose of his mission—to do good—was kept to with remarkable singleness of eye.    When pressed to visit palaces and picture galleries, or even to turn aside to witness special natural wonders, Mr. Shillitoe would courteously but firmly reply that he must be about his Master's business, for the time was short, his life far advanced, the work abundant, and the labourers in it very few.

His, too, was the vigilant eye for casual opportunities of usefulness, for the word " in season and out of season ; " for the dispersion of the wayside seed, "here a little, and there a little."   When travelling in the slow canal boats in Holland he distributed tracts, and relinquished the more comfortable saloon deck for the unpleasant tobacco-fumes of the close steerage, where he sought and found occasion for religious conversation with individuals and groups amongst the humbler passengers.

Similarly, when crossing the Atlantic, he used to invite his fellow-voyagers to assemble for reading the Scriptures and for collective worship, in which he abundantly preached the Gospel to them.

At meal-times he often availed himself of opportunities for useful and suggestive religious remarks.   He earnestly advocated the habit of assembling families for the daily reading of the Scriptures, and recommended an habitual pause before or after the reading, to afford facility for silent or vocal prayer, and for serious reflection.   Such pauses are often observed in the family Bible readings amongst the Friends.   When they are not merely momentary and formal in their duration, but *long enough for real usefulness* (as, for instance, five or ten minutes), they furnish most valuable " times of refreshing" for the spiritual needs of daily life. Thomas Shillitoe prized such pauses very highly. He used to say that they were acceptable feeding times for the soul, and that, feeling his need for all the religious strength he could obtain, he thankfully embraced these quiet breathing times amid the turmoil and exigencies of week-day engagements. Of course special rest, reflection, and edification on the Sabbath are most essential; but very beneficial also are these fragments of Sabbatic refreshment, when secured for distribution throughout the busy course of the six days following.

The writer has often recurred, with much satisfaction, to some time spent in a large household in Yorkshire, where the head habitually assembled the family twice every day for the reading of the Scriptures, and accompanied it, on each occasion, with from five to ten minutes' silence. The serious reflections and feelings of those daily gatherings were often highly beneficial to those who assembled, and greatly increased the improvement of the portions read. But merely reading the Bible, without having or taking opportunity for reflection and prayer, is of little, if any, real value for the actual and practical wants of the life of the soul.

Thomas Shillitoe, both at home and abroad, gave attention to *the economy of religious and moral effort;* that is to say, he directed special labour where it would be likely to produce the most extensive and abiding results. He took special interest in benefiting ministers, teachers, and all persons having much influence on the minds of others.

It has been said that every theological student is a legion in himself, so far as regards influence for good or for evil; at least, it is often so. Those who form the character of ministers, teachers, and public instructors, also form the characters of multitudes beside. So Mr. Shillitoe felt, and therefore laboured with special assiduity and prayer for the souls of such. For the good of young and, as yet, unformed minds, he also earnestly strove.

His favourable reception amongst strangers was greatly facilitated by the homeliness and outspoken heartiness of his manner, and by his unaffected cheerfulness. Like his intimate friend, the well known Peter Bedford,* he was a notable example of a person "good, without being disagreeable." When in Holland he received a letter from a worthy sensible woman of that country, in which she wrote:—"I am glad that Providence brought you into this country and to our town; and I hope that your way of discoursing with so much freeness and open-ness, will prove that the idea which is common amongst our Dutch people, that all Quakers are stiff people, will be taken away; and that the way in which you speak about religion will prove to them that though you are convinced that, in our speaking and not speaking, we are dependent on the Spirit of God, and we must always be looking to His influence, yet this makes none fanatics."

Thomas Shillitoe and Peter Bedford were both men of much humour. At times their cheerful spirits were even

---

* For an account of this very remarkable man, see a work published by S. W. Partridge, 9, Paternoster Row, London, entitled "*Peter Bedford, the Spitalfields Philanthropist,*" price 2s. 6d.

exuberant, and they seemed to take a delight in astonishing and good-temperedly shocking the unbending gravity of their Quaker compeers of the last generation, the unsympathetic stiffness of some of whom often obtained for their sect the estimation which the worthy Dutchwoman alluded to. Shillitoe would sometimes make the good Friends start by suddenly appearing amongst a group of them with a slap on the back of some one; and, on turning quickly around to see the disturber, there would appear the smiling face, bright eyes, and Roman nose of the dapper little Thomas. His friend Peter often indulged in similar fraternal freedoms.

Thomas, plain and homely as he was, was a great favourite with the women-folk, and, in his way, was exemplarily gallant and polite, especially to poor and hard-working females. His gallantry was like that of the courtly senator, who seeing, in Covent Garden Market, an Irishwoman striving in vain to raise a heavy basket on her shoulders, promptly lifted it for her, and received for thanks—" You're a *rale* gintleman, you are."

During his travels in Norway, Mr. Shillitoe on one occasion had been provided with two women to run beside his curricle, and take care of it and the horses, on a very rugged mountain route. The journey was peculiarly arduous; and the women were agreeably surprised when the good foreigner persisted in taking his turn with them in leading the horses, so as to allow of their riding. In mentioning the circumstance, he adds, " I believe we suffer ourselves to be plundered of much of that peace which a beneficent Almighty Creator designs for us in this life, through yielding to a selfish disposition of mind, and an unwillingness to take our share with others in the difficulties and inconveniences of life. Oh! may I ever remain willing that my luxuries in life may be given up in order to supply others' wants or comforts; and my comforts at times be given up to supply others' want of necessaries; and that even my necessaries, at times, may be given up to relieve the extreme distress of others, is what I crave, from the assurance that such conduct is consistent with the true Christian character."

On another occasion, when on a pedestrian mission in the South of Ireland, Thomas saw on the road before him a party of men and women going to market. An impression came over his mind that he ought to give them some good counsel. On overtaking the company he introduced his discourse by some cheerful remarks on the want of gallantry in Ireland, where the woman were left to carry the bundles and follow, whilst the men walked independently in front; whereas, he added, the latter ought to take the bundles, and offer their arms to the former. This discourse pleased the women much, and opened the way for a more general exhortation.

After traversing Holland, Mr. Shillitoe proceeded to Altona and Hamburg. Here he got into trouble, and for the first and last time in his life was taken into custody and locked up. Having observed with deep grief the general desecration of the Sabbath, and the prevalence of public immorality in the two towns, he drew up two earnest addresses to their inhabitants. These he sent to England to be printed, and on receiving a sufficient supply of copies, proceeded personally to deliver them in Altona, and also engaged three men to assist in the work of distribution there and in Hamburg. Whilst thus engaged, a young man of gentlemanly manners and appearance accosted him, and asked to be favoured with one of the documents he was issuing. On receiving it, and after some general conversation, he suddenly informed Mr. Shillitoe that it was his painful duty to arrest him and take him to the guard-house. Here Thomas was taken in charge by a police officer, and locked up till the next day in a cold, comfortless place, the stone floor of which was wet and very muddy. He requested permission to write to his friends in the town, but the favour was refused; neither was he permitted to send to his lodgings for his overcoat. A soldier, off duty, seeing the forlorn condition of the good Friend, took pity on him, and lent him his great-coat till his hour of duty came, when it had to be parted with, leaving Thomas more chilly than ever. When night arrived, some of his acquaintances, who had missed him, ascertained where he was, and came to offer themselves as bail for his re-appearance next day, if permitted to return to his lodgings for the night only. This was refused, and the prisoner was locked up in his place, with the prospect of the dirty wet floor to lie on. But better treatment was ultimately conceded, and his friends were permitted to bring him something hot for supper, two overcoats, and two chairs to lie on. Thus provided, he passed the night in comparative comfort. He writes, " My spirit was free, and far removed from the molestation of the police-master." Next morning his assiduous friends sent him a good breakfast of chocolate and cake, after which he was marched off to the police-master's court. That functionary, however, appeared much embarrassed with his prisoner's case, and continued to pace backwards and forwards, muttering to himself, a considerable time, whilst he kept Thomas waiting. At length he announced that, from respect to the position of the friends of the latter in Hamburg, he should discharge him, and thus the good man was speedily released from his durance vile.

The addresses could not have been really objectionable, or in any way injudicious, inasmuch as two days after his discharge by the chief police-officer of Altona, the principal magistrate of Hamburg, on whom Mr. Shillitoe now waited, told him that he had read each of the addresses with much satisfaction, and added, "You have done our city a great kindness by their circulation; I have no doubt but, in time, fruits will appear; but the amendment so necessary amongst us must be a gradual work." He further, speaking for himself and the other authorities of Hamburg, said, "Take up your abode with us at Hamburg; we esteem your character and motives for coming amongst us, assured, as we are, of the purity of your intentions, and that nothing but true love could have influenced you to have done as you have done: you needed no certificate from your friends; you have already given us the best certificate yourself."

The same day Thomas walked back to Altona, where he found that his arrest had drawn general attention to his address, much more so than would otherwise have been the case; so that his temporary annoyance was overruled for much good. Next day he called on the Governor of Altona, who had been absent from the town at the time of his arrest, and who now courteously apologized to him for the occurrence. The pastor of one of the principal churches there made the address the subject of a sermon, confirming the truth of its statements, and expressing deep regret that a foreigner should have found occasion to call the inhabitants to so just an account for their wickedness.

After some further religious labour in Hamburg, Thomas Shillitoe proceeded to Copenhagen and other parts of Denmark. Here he underwent much inconvenience from the tempestuous rainy weather, and from his ignorance of any language but English. At one place, after a fast of many hours, he arrived at a tavern, where he requested some hot milk to mix with a bottle of thick chocolate he had brought in his pocket. Weak with the long fast, he reeled against a table, and smashed the bottle, the contents of which flowed through and over his dress, by no means improving his appearance. The woman of the house stared stupidly at her visitor, but offered no assistance to help him in his muddle. As he had no other suit of clothes, he was anxious speedily to cleanse them, and, making signs to be conducted to the kitchen, there procured some water, with which he managed to remove part of the greasy mess from his garments.

Whilst waiting for some more breakfast he observed a person tying up his carpet-bag and trunk with tape, and innocently supposed that the latter having perhaps fallen open, the stranger was kindly refastening it for him. But presently he ascertained that his luggage, having been now sealed with the custom-house seal, was to be taken from him until he reached Kiel, where it would be examined.

F

A week or two afterwards Mr. Shillitoe was in Copenhagen, and in the course of some arrangements for a
religious interview with the King of Denmark, the Prime
Minister, observing the greasy condition of his clothes,
very naturally exclaimed with astonishment, "You do not
mean to appear before His Majesty in those clothes, do
you?" Thomas, with his usual honest simplicity, remarked that he had no others with him, that his summer
garments were left at Altona, and he was about to procure
winter ones on his arrival in Norway. The Count smiled.
But Thomas went before the King, and, in spite of soiled
garments, had an interview very interesting and satisfactory both to the monarch and his humble visitor.

In the same clothes also, Thomas had very agreeable
interviews with the Queen and Princesses of Denmark.

His reception at Copenhagen amply compensated for
the "sore bones and bruised flesh" which his rough
journey thither had inflicted on him.

The contemplation of winter travel in Sweden and Norway was to him a very serious matter. But faith sustained
him in a cheerful hope and prayerful trust; and he wrote,
"I must be content to live one day at a time, avoiding all
unnecessary anxiety about the morrow."

He now advertised for a courier, acquainted with Norwegian and Swedish travel, to conduct him to Christiania,
but could obtain no one except a rogue of a black man,
whose character was as dark as his skin. Thomas records
that this was "as wicked, dark a spirit as I ever before
had met with." At their first interview, his terms were
so exorbitant, and his appraisement of his own virtues so
high, that he was dismissed for the present. Meanwhile,

no one else could be heard of. The season was advancing, and a speedy start was necessary. Mr. Shillitoe pondered the matter very seriously. He remembered how God had cared for him when he first left his home on a Gospel mission, and how the drunken foreman had then been temporarily constrained to extraordinary carefulness and efficiency. So it might be now, if prayer and faith were exercised. The Lord could restrain this evil guide from doing mischief to his employer. At length, very reluctantly, the negro was engaged; and during the ten days of travel which elapsed between Copenhagen and Christiania, although he manifested himself as a drunken, swearing, and dishonest fellow, yet eventually things turned out much better than might have been expected. On the route they had also many difficulties to encounter, owing to the deep snow, thick fogs, rugged routes, and intense cold. Thus (in Sweden) they frequently broke their harness, many times in a day, and lost their linch-pins. The latter casualty, however, was speedily remedied whenever it occurred, by the driver substituting a stick from the hedge, and proceeding, with no apparent fear of danger, close to the edge of steep precipices and deep waters. Thomas was very glad, indeed, to reach Christiania, and so get quit of his vicious and miserable conductor. He notes that immediately after his arrival there the heavy rains set in, which were followed by hard frosts, which rendered the route he had just arrived by no longer passable. He, therefore, very reasonably considered that his procedure had been providentially timed and ruled.

In Christiania and other places in Norway, Thomas

Shillitoe paid a number of visits to ministers, students, and persons of influence, also to the criminals in prison. Being in Christiania during the festivities of New Year's Day, his quiet was much disturbed, even in his lodgings, by the numerous persons who came to visit the house. He, therefore, withdrew himself to a solitary apartment, but there his tranquillity was rudely broken in upon by a rush of roystering masqueraders, who burst in upon him, and for a time produced a scene of uproarious jollity, which Thomas (understanding neither their language nor customs) regarded with dumb disgust and pity. He was much grieved at the prevalence in Norway of Sabbath dancing parties, a custom defended and united in by many even of the Lutheran clergy.

The magnificent scenery of Norway naturally excited his profound admiration, and, contrary to his usual custom, he inserted in his memoranda in that country, occasional expressions of his appreciation of its beauties, praising "the stupendous mountains, rising one above the other to the clouds,—a vast expanse of sea in prospect, in different directions,—the sun warming the earth with his silvery beams, and scarcely a cloud to be seen in the bold horizon,—the numerous land and water fowls appearing in the full enjoyment of those blessings their beneficent Creator has bestowed upon them." Elsewhere he writes of a place named Devick, near Lundale, "A more beautiful retreat from the hurries of this world I thought I never before had met with. I could not but persuade myself I might be warranted, in degree, in comparing it with the abode of our first parents,—beautifully wooded and watered, abounding with birds of various kinds, whose shrill and melodious voices echoed in the air; the ground also appeared so fertile as not to require much labour to produce food for the inhabitants and their cattle; but I had not explored its inhabitants. When this took place, I do not know that I was ever more disgusted at any time of my life, than with the slothful appearance of the inhabitants, our captain's family excepted, both in their houses and their land, but, above all, in their persons." Mr. Shillitoe with difficulty had these slothful folks gathered together; and he then preached to them a thoroughly practical, vigorous, plain-spoken sermon, telling them his sorrow at their indolence and neglect, and enforcing on them the duties of industry and cleanliness, and especially of bringing up their children in tidy and active habits. The people listened attentively, but were densely crowded, to the annoyance of Mr. Shillitoe, who remarks, "We were obliged to pack very close together. My next neighbour was so frequently rubbing and scratching herself during the meeting, my mind was for a time somewhat disturbed by it, expecting I should have some of the company that were the cause of her exertions."

Of one of the numerous fiords, he records, "Our passage up the river Seroog was awfully grand; in some places the pass was so straight between the rocks that we barely made our way along; in other places the huge mass of rock appeared suspended above our heads as if ready to fall, many pieces of the same lying in the river."

From Norway Mr. Shillitoe proceeded to Prussia and other parts of Germany, where he had interviews with many persons in authority, and held religious meetings with companies of serious individuals. One of these was held under circumstances of peculiar disadvantage, for a meeting commencing with silence, after the usual manner of the Friends. It was at a farm-house, where the most suitable place for such a gathering was in the large entrance hall in the centre of the establishment, and around which were ranged stalls for the cattle, above which ran a gallery containing the apartments of the family. In the stalls were a horse, a cow, calves, pigs, a goat, and poultry. These manifesting no indications of quietness, but the reverse, the visitor at first inclined to relinquish the idea of a meeting; but as a company had assembled, and as there was no better place (it being rainy and muddy out of doors), they endeavoured to settle down. He describes it thus, "We took our seats together; soon after which the cow put out her head, and gave a loud bellow, and the pigs and geese became very noisy. This interruption to our quiet continued for some time, when, to my great surprise, all at once became quiet, as much so as if there had not been a living creature near beside ourselves; which quiet continued until the meeting was over." The animals appeared awed and hushed by the unusual and protracted stillness of the human company in their midst.

By the aid of interpreters and translations, Mr. Shillitoe was far more successful than could have been expected in his Continental ministrations, in spite of his entire ignorance of any language but his own. In Switzerland he had a peculiarly interesting interview with a deeply pious gentleman, who chiefly communicated with him by the language of signs. Finding that they could not converse in the ordinary way, the Swiss, by placing his hand first on his own heart, and then on Mr. Shillitoe's breast, gave the latter to understand that they could feel a communion of spirit which they could not express. Then fetching from his library a large volume of copperplates, illustrating the Gospels and the life of our Lord, he signified by various gestures at certain scenes there depicted his appreciation of the offices of Christ and of His Spirit. In particular, at the plate representing our Lord casting out devils from the herd of swine, he succeeded in giving Mr. Shillitoe to understand that, at the present time, Christ still performs a similar miracle in the hearts of sinful men who prayerfully and obediently seek Him. He then brought a map of England, and signified his wish to know from what locality his visitor came. Mr. Shillitoe then gave him a document in German, which he had with him, explaining the objects of his mission. This the Swiss gentleman read attentively, after which he paused in solemn silence, and, presently kneeling down, prayed with much fervency and earnestuess, evidently for a blessing on his visitor and his religious labours. Both wept freely in the depth of their sympathetic emotion, and taking leave of Mr. Shillitoe, the stranger clasped him long and affectionately in his arms, as if reluctant to part. The good Friend felt this hearty and congenial reception to be " like a brook by the way, cheering my drooping spirits."

After other visits to various places in Switzerland and France, Mr. Shillitoe returned to England in April 1823, after an absence of twenty-two months on his missionary travels on the Continent.

# CHAPTER V.

### FURTHER FOREIGN MISSIONS—RUSSIA AND AMERICA.

SECOND CONTINENTAL JOURNEY AND ITS LABOURS—SIX
MONTHS IN PETERSBURG—DANIEL WHEELER—DREAD OF
THE POLICE AND THE RATS—AWFUL INUNDATION AT
PETERSBURG—PERILOUS JOURNEY HOMEWARD—BERLIN—
RECRUITS HIS EXHAUSTED ENERGIES AT BUXTON—SEIZES
AN OPPORTUNITY OF USEFULNESS THERE, AND VISITS THE
DUKE OF DEVONSHIRE ON BEHALF OF THE POOR—EMBARKS
FOR AMERICA—THE HICKSITES—THE MORAL SENSE—INDIS-
PENSABLE NEED OF THE GOSPEL AND THE HOLY SCRIPTURES
—ADDRESS TO INDIANS AT CATARAGUS—TESTIMONIES OF
MR. MOFFATT AND OTHER MISSIONARIES AS TO THE NECES-
SITY OF THE BIBLE AND OF MINISTRY TO THE HEATHEN—
HAI EBN YOKDAN—"A CUMBER-GROUND"—CHILDREN AND
DOGS AT MEETING—VISITS TO THE PRESIDENT AND TO
SLAVE-OWNERS—RETURN TO ENGLAND.

AFTER a year's repose Mr. Shillitoe started for another
Continental journey in 1824, intending to visit other parts
of Germany, Denmark, and Prussia, and then to winter
in Russia, where he contemplated special religious engagements in Petersburg. As on his previous journey, his
labours consisted mainly of efforts for promoting Sabbath
observance, temperance, the welfare of prisoners, the
religious growth of serious individuals or small groups of
earnest Christians, and interviews with monarchs, nobles,
and magistrates.

His stay at Petersburg extended over six months, from September, 1824, to the end of February, 1825. During this period he had two very interesting interviews with the pious Emperor Alexander the First, and visited the prisons and other public institutions, in addition to his labours with private individuals. His stay in the Russian Metropolis was rendered much more pleasant than it would otherwise have been, by the frequent hospitalities extended to him by a family of English Quakers, named Wheeler, who resided a few miles out of the city, at a place named Shoosharry. The head of the family, Mr. Daniel Wheeler, had once been a soldier, but becoming acquainted with the Friends had left the army, and united himself to that body. By his industry and probity he had acquired a comfortable position in life, and had, a few years previously to Mr. Shillitoe's visit to Russia, come thither to reside as a superintendent of extensive agricultural operations, carried on at the special desire of the Emperor on one of the Imperial estates. When Alexander visited England with the allied monarchs, at the close of the wars with Napoleon, he had come into contact, on several occasions, with members of the Society of Friends, and especially with the excellent Mr. William Allen, head of the chemical firm of Allen, Hanbury and Howard, of Lombard Street, a universal philanthropist, once styled by Lord Brougham, "the best man in London." The Emperor was so pleased with Allen and some of his brother Friends, that he expressed a wish that some of their community might settle in Russia, and when, a few years afterwards, the works at Shoosharry were in contemplation, Alexander caused enquiry to be made for an

English Quaker as superintendent, rather than any one else. Mr. Wheeler offered himself, and was readily accepted. He, like Mr. Shillitoe, was an eminent preacher amongst the Friends, and after performing his work at Petersburg, under Alexander and his successor Nicholas, devoted the remainder of his life to long and arduous missionary journeys in Australia, Tasmania, the Islands of the Pacific Ocean, and the Continent of North America.

After the visit of the Emperor Alexander to England, he received several religious visits from Mr. Allen and another Quaker preacher (quite as remarkable for his extensive missionary travels), a Frenchman by birth, Mr. Stephen Grellet. The Emperor treated these good men with almost fraternal kindness, and corresponded for years with them through the medium of his private secretary, Prince Alexander Galitzin, who also was a truly religious person.

Thus, when Mr. Shillitoe arrived in Petersburg, he found that Quakers were well known at Court, and highly esteemed. But, at first, the police and subordinate officials were, for some time, very suspicious of the homely looking little Englishman. His steps were dogged by spies, and rumours were current in the city that he had been travelling all over the Continent, and everywhere giving away money freely, with a view, as was presumed, of some ultimate revolutionary project.

Mr. Shillitoe did not lodge with his kind friends, the Wheelers, but at a house in the heart of Petersburg; and when he ascertained the reports which were thus current respecting him, he became apprehensive of sudden arrest, and even, possibly, of secret deportation to Siberia. At any rate it seemed not unlikely but that he might be thrown into a dungeon as a spy or revolutionary emissary ; and the Emperor, to whom Mr. Wheeler could have satisfactorily explained the nature of his friend's mission and character, had not yet returned to Petersburg from an absence in the provinces. So Thomas, always apt to be nervous, now became more so than usual, and Mr. Wheeler, who was a man of humour and keenly enjoyed a joke, could not refrain from pleasantly contributing to his ideas of the terrors of Russian dungeons, by telling him of the multitude of hungry rats frequenting them. Poor Mr. Shillitoe gravely entered his dismal fears in his memoranda, and anxiously dwelt upon the prospect of their realization in his own experience.

Eventually he escaped all molestation by police or rats, and left Petersburg, after receiving marks of high honour from the Emperor and some of his grandees, as well as from the humbler objects of his labours.

But, in the interval, he witnessed an appalling catastrophe.

On the 19th of November, 1824, the city and vicinity of Petersburg were visited by an inundation of unparalleled magnitude, which resulted in an awful destruction of life and property. On starting to take his usual walk after breakfast, Mr. Shillitoe was surprised at finding his lodgings so surrounded by water, that he speedily returned and told his landlady that they were living on an island. Not understanding him, she merely smiled. Presently Mr. Shillitoe observed wading across the yard a servant of an English lady who lodged in the same establishment, and who was already overtaken by the now rapidly rising

waters.    Higher and higher the flood deepened, until men
were up to their necks, and horses and carriages swimming
in the streets, where there was soon twelve feet of water.
The ground-floor of Mr. Shillitoe's lodging was occupied
by a grocer's shop.    This was filled from floor to ceiling,
and still the flood continued gradually rising, until it was
feared the houses would be wholly submerged, and their
inhabitants drowned together.

In the court-yard of Mr. Shillitoe's house, a poor man
was floated on the top of a carriage under an archway,
where he was in danger of being drowned.    He raised
piercing cries, but it was two hours before any one was
able to extricate him from his dangerous position.    Mr.
Shillitoe could not help him, but suffered much from the
sight of his jeopardy, and from his shrieks for help.    A
horse also, attached to a small cart, swam outside Mr.
Shillitoe's windows, and with difficulty kept its head above
water, by planting its fore-feet on the top of a flight of
steps.    In this position it continued several hours, when
a policeman came in a boat to its aid.    From ten o'clock
till four in the afternoon, there prevailed the most awful
stillness.    Not a person was seen to stir.    Towards
evening the waters were evidently sinking; and, as they
retired, they burst open doors and windows, threw down
walls and houses, and did immense mischief.    That night
was one of awful darkness and stillness, no lamps being
lighted, as it was impracticable to attempt it.

On the following day the flood had left the streets, and
it was possible to walk abroad in some directions and
witness the effects of the calamity.    Many of the bridges
were carried away.    All were injured.    Many houses were

wholly swept away. In one row of cottages 250 corpses were found. Multitudes of horses and cattle perished. For miles around the city fences were washed away, and the fields covered with fragments of houses, broken furniture, timber, and dead bodies of men and beasts.

Mr. Wheeler and his family had happily escaped injury, their dwelling being on elevated ground.

Thomas Shillitoe continued in Petersburg three months after this terrible flood. In the spring following he returned overland through Prussia and Germany to his native country. On this journey he suffered many inconveniences from the cold weather, the deep mud of the woods, the danger of crossing rivers choked with fragments of broken ice, and, at times, the discomforts of unpleasant sleeping quarters, especially in Russia and East Prussia. Thus he mentions that when near Marienburg the wheels of their vehicle repeatedly sunk into deep mud-holes, which all but overturned them. Then, after crossing two frozen rivers in the dark, they came to a region which was so widely flooded that their course had to be changed from time to time in all directions, east, west, north, and south, to avoid the deeper tracts of water surrounding them; then other rivers to cross; and the next night at a village on the banks of the Vistula, no lodging-place but the dirty floor of a room covered with pea-stalks.

Mr. Shillitoe thus describes the scene :—" On entering this room where we had to take up our lodging for the night, dirty-looking miserable men and women put their heads out of the pea-straw to gaze on us; others were drinking, smoking, and making a noise; clean straw was brought in for us, upon which I could gladly have laid

down my weary bones, but for fear of damp and the
vermin I might collect from my next neighbour, as they
were lying pretty thickly about the floor, except where
others were sitting, drinking, and smoking; we concluded
to keep on our fur-coats, and, by the help of a table to
lay our heads upon, to try to get some sleep. Towards
morning we enjoyed some quiet, and at day-break a pretty
general sallying out took place of men and women. Some
of the men proceeded to prepare the way through the ice
for our departure. I rejoiced to see the peep of day, and
was glad to turn out of our filthy apartment, and get away
from the fumes of the spirits and tobacco, to breathe the
fresh air; but when we came to take a view by daylight
of the road which we had travelled to reach this miserable
abode, and the danger we had been exposed to, whilst it
occasioned a chill of dread all over me, it awakened afresh
in my mind such feelings of gratitude as caused songs of
praise sweetly to arise to that Almighty Power who had
thus in mercy watched over us, and preserved us from all
harm."

Moving westward through Prussia and Germany, and
staying at Berlin and other cities where opportunities of
religious usefulness opened, Mr. Shillitoe again reached
home.

His arduous labours and long travels had, at his
advanced age, produced much weariness and lassitude.
His friends therefore recommended him to recruit for a
few weeks amid the quiet scenery of Derbyshire, and to
drink the waters and bathe in the baths at Buxton. But
weakly and in repose, he was still alive to every opportunity of usefulness. Whilst at Buxton he, one day,

stepped into the bathing-place allotted to poor men, but found it so small, so miserably deficient in ventilation, and in such bad condition generally, that he was glad to quit it hastily. He was informed that many of these poor patients caught severe colds from the insufficient accommodation, and from often having to remain naked on bare stone seats and benches, and then to dress without the use of towels. On enquiry, Mr. Shillitoe finding that the agent of the Duke of Devonshire (the owner of the baths) had already had his attention drawn to the gross neglect of the poor, but had never taken means to remedy it, felt it his duty to lay the matter in person before the Duke, who was then staying at Chatsworth. Thither Thomas walked, a distance of twelve miles. On arriving at the porter's lodge he was informed that he could not see the Duke. Not to be repulsed he took from his pocket a religious book, and sent with it the following note, which he wrote to introduce it and himself :—

" One of the Society of Friends wishes in person to present the Duke with a work, which he hopes the Duke will find an interest in reading."

The note was sent in, and Thomas was requested to follow. The Duke received him very courteously, and on offering to pay for the book, Thomas of course refused to receive any money, but at once stated the real and main object of his coming—to plead for the neglected poor at Buxton. He asked further permission to read to the Duke a detailed report of the abuses which he had drawn up and brought with him. The Duke, after listening attentively to it, entered freely into conversation, and expressed his obligation for the pains Mr. Shillitoe had taken to lay the matter before him.

Thankful and satisfied at the result of his effort, Thomas walked back again to Buxton, although the weather was very hot and his health indifferent.

The Duke's agent, on hearing of his journey to Chatsworth, called on him and stated that, if he had laid the matter before himself instead of troubling the Duke with it, the matter should have been attended to. But Thomas was better satisfied to apply at head-quarters and at the fountain source of power. Soon afterwards the Duke gave orders to effect all needful improvements in the baths for poor men and women; and they were accordingly rendered much more comfortable.

After a few months spent in the bosom of his family, Thomas Shillitoe again started for extensive foreign service in his Divine Master's work. This time it was to America.

He embarked at Liverpool for New York in the autumn of 1826 (at the age of seventy-two). On the voyage thither (of about six weeks) he exerted himself in many ways to promote the religious improvement of his fellow-passengers. In his diary on board occurs the following brief prayer:—

"O, Holy Father! keep me in the hollow of Thy Divine hand this day; that so, through my good example to the multitude enclosed with me by these wooden walls, who appear watching my movements, Thy great name may be glorified, and inquiry begotten after the more acceptable way of serving Thee, our God."

His American journey occupied more than three years. Much of it was taken up in visiting the meetings of his fellow-members of the Society of Friends, who at that period were undergoing a sort of religious revolution, by the secession of some eighty thousand of their body, who formed themselves into a separate association, usually named that of the Hicksites, after their leader and chief preacher, Elias Hicks, of Jericho, on Long Island. Most of Mr. Shillitoe's memoranda made during his American travel, relate to matters connected with these sectarian differences, and which therefore only call for a general notice.

The Hicksites not only asserted that they were the legitimate successors, in faith and doctrine, of George Fox and his contemporaries, but they also at first claimed Thomas Shillitoe as a virtual adherent of their party. But in this they were mistaken, for he vigorously protested against them.

They went sad lengths. They denied the special inspiration and paramount authority of the Bible; they rejected the doctrines of the Deity and sacrificial atonement of our Lord Jesus Christ; they declared that every man has within him an "inward light" wholly sufficient in itself to guide him into salvation, independently of the Bible, or of instruction in the facts of the Gospels. In their doctrine they may be said to have virtually dispensed with the Son of God, by denying His deity, incarnation, and propitiatory sacrifice as "a ransom for all." Professing special reverence for the Holy Spirit, they habitually and particularly dishonoured His own great gift of the Holy Scriptures, by systematic disparagement,

G

and by virtually degrading them to the level of ordinary human works.    In short, the Hicksites trampled on some of the common fundamentals of the Christian faith.

Yet they did so in many cases from an honest perversion of principles in which they had been educated.   Some of their views did naturally result from the doctrines which certain well-meaning persons of a former generation had promulgated amongst them in books early familiar to them.

A principal source of their delusion arose from the controversy respecting the responsibility of the heathen. They assumed that, inasmuch as scores of millions of these have never received the Bible, or heard of a Saviour, therefore there must be, in accordance with Divine justice, a universal manifestation of the Holy Spirit granted them sufficient to save without Gospel or minister.    They asserted that such a universal light is found in every heathen person.    But here they mistook the common moral sense for such a saving light.    It is true that all men have, in greater or less degree, a moral sense ; or, in other words, something within which testifies a certain measure of approval of right and disapproval of wrong. Even the beasts have a degree of such a moral sense. Thus, a cat, which has stolen meat from the cook, betrays by its demeanour a sense of conviction.    Still more do dogs, after disobeying their owners, testify (by their slinking aspect, their ears thrown back, and tails drawn between their legs,) a keen sense of wrong and shame. The elephant has been known to commit suicide after, in a fit of passion, killing its master and feeder.    On the other hand, these animals, especially the dog, manifest a lively sense of self-approval after rendering special fidelity and service to their owners. Hence they are said to have a sort of moral sense. And so have all men, even the lowest savages, in smaller or greater measure.

But such a moral sense is an entirely different gift from the glorious and sanctifying presence of the Holy Spirit, a presence producing affections and feelings which universal experience proves only to be accorded in connection with the teachings of scriptural revelation, and the typical or fulfilled manifestations of God's holiness and love in Jesus Christ our Lord. In all ages and in all lands it has been found that there has been no individual or national holiness, nothing approaching to virtue or goodness in its higher aspects, apart from the possession of an outward Revelation. For the love of God can only spring from the knowledge of Him. Where, as in the case of a very few of the Greeks and Romans, considerable approaches toward virtue were manifested, there is good reason for concluding that indirectly some of the truths derived from God's revelation to the Jews and to the Prophets had reached these under modified and almost unrecognizable forms.

It has been justly remarked by President Jonathan Edwards, in his " Miscellaneous Observations,"—" What instance can be mentioned from any history of any one nation under the sun that emerged from atheism or idolatry into the knowledge or adoration of the one true God, without the assistance of Revelation? The Americans, the Africans, the Tartars, and the ingenious Chinese, have had time enough, one would think, to find out the right and true idea of God; and yet, after about five thousand years' improvement, and the full exercise of reason, they have, at this day, got no farther in their progress towards the true religion than to the worship of stocks and stones and devils."

But the Hicksites ignored the real experiences of heathendom, and proclaimed that, in the mere dim moral sense, common to all men, and shared in even by some beasts, these possessed the sacred gift of the Holy Spirit, and were safe for Heaven and salvation without Bibles and without preachers. By a natural and consistent inference, they have reasoned that if the Bible and outward preaching were not necessary to bring the heathen to Heaven, neither were they indispensable for civilized persons such as themselves. They utterly confounded two distinct questions, namely, the necessity for a knowledge of the Gospel of Christ to produce the fruits of the Holy Spirit, and the problem of the future condition of those who have never received either. They were not content to believe, "Shall not the Judge of all the earth do right?" but asserted a great many other things contrary alike to experience and to Scripture. Eventually they went further, and denied the authority and standard both of the Scriptures and of Christ.

Many of Elias Hicks' assertions are too blasphemous for quotation ; but it was his habit to speak of the blessed Bible as "a mere written book," and to declare that innate ideas, or an intuitional sense, afforded the chief knowledge of God and of Christ. He proclaimed, "It is a great truth that what is to be known of God is manifested *only in* man. *There* is the place that He manifests Himself.

In like manner one of the first systematic writers on Deism, Lord Herbert of Cherbury, wrote with much plausible sincerity,—" We come at the knowledge of Divine things by innate ideas, or by having the law and rule of life written and engraven on our hearts in such plain visible characters, that whoever looks into himself will clearly discern the great principles and duties of religion."

These teachings ignored the inspired declarations, that all men are in darkness until the love of God in Christ is revealed to them by the preaching of the Gospel and the perusal of Holy Scripture. The Psalmist proclaims, " The *entrance* of *Thy words* giveth light " (Ps. cxix. 130). And the Apostle Paul was not sent to direct the Gentiles to the light of innate ideas, or of a mere moral sense ; but received the commission from Christ personally,—" I send thee to open their eyes, and to turn them *from darkness* to light, and from the power of Satan unto God." Thus, too, he told the Ephesians that they had been " dead in trespasses and sins," but had received light through his apostolic message respecting Christ, in whom ye also trusted *after that ye heard* the word of truth, the *Gospel* of your salvation."

Yet it was not altogether without some reason that the Hicksites at first claimed Thomas Shillitoe as a partial supporter of their views. For although in his own life he earnestly honoured the Holy Scriptures as the great rule of faith and practice, yet there had on certain occasions escaped from him ambiguous teachings on the subject, and especially in an address issued by him whilst in America to the Seneca tribe of Indians assembled at Cataragus.

The tenour of his address on that occasion was by no means so clear and scriptural as his usual exhortations. A measure of sectarian opposition to certain missionaries appears to have then led him into expressions which after-wards caused regret and pain to his Christian friends.

In this address he said,—"I now declare, that so far from my believing the Scriptures to be the only means of salvation and sole rule for our conduct, I am decidedly opposed to such dangerous and false opinions on such important subjects as these are. I consider them to be the writings of holy men in former ages, who were inspired by the Great Spirit ; and that they contain good counsel and advice. But, brothers, I consider such as tell you that they are the only rule or means of salvation, to be under the influence of a wrong spirit. I believe such missionaries have made a wrong use of these writings."

In these words Mr. Shillitoe, truly good man as he was, unintentionally, but virtually, endorsed the root principle of Hicksism. In all ages of Christendom it has been found that religious and social progress has made way in precisely the same proportion in which the Bible has been acknowledged as the only safe standard of faith and doctrine, and in proportion as it has been prayer-fully depended on as the guiding star of life ; even as our holy Redeemer declared, " The *words* which I speak unto you, they are spirit, and they are life." And again He says, " Ye are clean through the *word which I have spoken* unto you."

Thomas, with all his virtues, had his many weak points, like other men. Although generally good tempered and lively, he could manifest much acerbity when provoked.

On one occasion, at a great meeting of Quakers in London, he became so excited and violent towards some person who differed from him, that, aged man and experienced minister as he then was, two of the Friends were necessitated to take hold of him and lead him away forcibly from the scene of conflict. And a few weeks before his decease, one of the last letters, if not the very last, which his intimate friend, Peter Bedford, wrote to him, was a loving exhortation not to let his irritability at opposition manifest itself too strongly. Thomas was very sensible of his defect in this respect, and sometimes alluded to it in his memoranda and letters. Thus, on one occasion, speaking of the virtue of patience, he candidly adds that it is " an ingredient I have very little of in my natural composition."

Another reason why the Hicksites erroneously laid claim to him as an adherent is to be found in a feature of his preaching, which was certainly a frequent defect in it. Mr. Shillitoe, although very zealous for public morality, for temperance, for reverent observance of the sabbath, and for other moral and religious duties, was not equally urgent in laying the axe at the *root* of the tree of evil. He did not perceive so habitually as was needful, that it is only from the love of Christ that good works can flow as natural and permanent fruit, rather than as forced and transient efforts.

Although at the close of his life he boldly and humbly pleaded the merits and sufferings of the Lord Jesus as his only trust for heaven, yet it is but fair to acknowledge that in his general ministry there was not the like full and prominent recognition of the love of God as displayed in the incarnation of the Lord Jesus, our infinitely compassionate

Redeemer, to the thorough extent which Scripture truth requires. There was certainly a want of more emphatic and habitual reference to the sacred " blood of sprinkling " in his sermons. Hence, again, the Hicksites looked toward him at first as to a somewhat favourable sympathizer with their own radically defective doctrines.

The question of the heathen and their innate ideas as sufficient for salvation, was, on various occasions, taken up by Mr. Shillitoe during his American visit, and he certainly compromised himself, in degree, by endorsing some of the views of the Hicksites on the subject, and by appearing to disparage the Holy Scriptures. Yet, those who really knew his life and heartfelt convictions, were convinced of his virtual reverence for the Scriptures as the rule of faith. But his trumpet at times gave a decidedly uncertain sound. Hence trouble ensued. Some of his meetings during the Hicksite controversy were times of downright riot. He had once or twice to flee from fear of violence. But these painful scenes we shall pass by.

It is, however, appropriate here to introduce one or two testimonies, by experienced Christian missionaries, as to the non-existence of any really efficacious innate principles in the heathen, apart from, or antecedent to, their reception of the outward and historic facts of Christ's love and incarnation as set forth in the Holy Scriptures.

The excellent Robert Moffatt, in his " Missionary Labours in South Africa," written after forty years of Christian labour amongst the heathen there, says of them, " Their ignorance, though to a calm reasoner on the subject not to be wondered at, was distressing in the extreme, and perfectly confounding to my preconceived notions about innate and intuitive ideas, and what some term natural light."—(p. 32, 20th edition.) He adds (p. 64) "While Satan is obviously the author of the polytheism of other nations, he has employed his agency with fatal success in erasing every vestige of religious impression from the minds of the Bechuanas, Hottentots, and Bushmen, leaving them *without a single ray* to guide them." Mr. Campbell says of these heathen, "They looked on the sun with the eyes of an ox." Mr. Moffatt further records, of a converted and specially intelligent heathen, "The question being put to one whose memory was tenacious, as his judgment was enlightened, 'How did you feel upon retiring, from private as well as public crimes, and laying your head on the silent pillow? Were there no fears in your breast, no spectres before your eyes, no conscience accusing you of having done wrong; no palpitations, no dread of futurity?' 'No,' said he, 'How could we feel, or how could we fear? We had no idea that an unseen eye saw us, or that an unseen ear heard us. What could we know beyond ourselves, or of another world, before life and immortality were brought to us by the word of God.' This declaration was followed by a flood of tears; while he added, 'You found us beasts and not men.'"

A similar testimony is borne by Mr. Henry Nott, one of the earliest missionaries to the South Seas, respecting the universal absence of the glorious gifts of the Holy Ghost amongst the tribes destitute of the Gospel of Jesus Christ.

The scriptural declarations are, that "where there is

no law there is no transgression;" "As many as have sinned without law shall also perish without law;" and "He who knew not his Lord's will, and committed deeds worthy of stripes, shall be beaten with few stripes."

The Bible declares that the heathen will *not be punished* for what they have never received; but that, nevertheless, they cannot be qualified for the glories of heaven except by the sanctifying discipline of the Spiritual influences flowing from the revelation of God's love in Jesus Christ, the Holy One once bleeding on the Cross for the sins of all men, and now risen on high, until He come again to establish His everlasting kingdom with the saints, a kingdom into which only sanctified and redeemed persons will be permitted to enter; those who have, through faith and prayerful obedience, obtained the prize, the glorious *gift* of eternal life, from Christ.

Mr. Moffatt impressively concludes :—" The Apostle Paul, feeling the full weight of the Saviour's commission, adds to the fearful list of iniquities and flagitious sins, committed by his own countrymen, the Jews, that of forbidding him and his colleagues ' to preach to the Gentiles *that they might be saved*.' Thus, if the apostle is to be our example, and if the commands of the Saviour are to be our guide, our duty is as plain as if written by a noontide ray, to make known to perishing heathen, whether at home or abroad, the words of eternal life."

Mr. Shillitoe himself was a most devoted practical illustration of this apostolic zeal in promulgating religious truth. He was willing to spend and be spent in the service, and had consecrated himself, as a living sacrifice unto God, for its accomplishment. The Hicksites, as

might be expected, left the heathen in their native darkness, to the light of their falsely-presumed innate ideas.
But so did not Mr. Shillitoe.  And so did not George
Fox, whom the Hicksites professed to follow.  He tra-
versed sea and land, mountain and wilderness, to preach
the Gospel.  After he had aroused persons to spiritual
earnestness for their own salvation, he urgently commanded them to teach others also.  Thus, to his brethren
in America, he wrote (in 1679), "All Friends, everywhere, that have Indians or blacks, you *are* to preach the
Gospel to them and other servants, *if you be true Christians;* for the Gospel of salvation was to be preached to
'*every* creature under heaven.'  Christ commands it to
His disciples, 'Go and teach all nations; baptizing them
into the name of the Father, Son, and Holy Ghost.'"

George Fox, in his mission incitements, specially connected the blessed gift of the Holy Spirit with the presence of the Gospel of the New Testament.  He wrote
again, "You *must* teach and instruct blacks, and Indians,
and others, how that God doth pour out of His Spirit
upon all flesh in these days of the New Covenant and
New Testament; and also you must instruct and teach
your Indians, and negroes, and all others, how that Christ,
by the grace of God, tasted death for every man, and
*gave Himself a ransom* for all men, to be testified in due
time."

This charge was truly scriptural, and it is to be wished
that good Mr. Shillitoe, with his usual zeal, had as clearly
acted upon it to the Seneca Indians.

Many score of pages of his memoranda are devoted to
recording the painful scenes of the Hicksite separation and

heresy. Before passing from them altogether, it may
appropriately be mentioned that the chief actual "fact,"
quoted as a practical proof in support of their doctrine of
heathen salvation through innate ideas, had been found to
be utterly spurious and fictitious. It was a narrative gravely
recorded by a learned writer, named Robert Barclay, in
all the earlier editions of his work entitled the "Apology,"
and was confidingly quoted by him from a translation of
an Arabic history of one Hai Eben Yokdan, who, as it
was alleged, when an infant, was thrown into the sea by
an unfortunate mother, but was carried by the waves, the
same night, to an uninhabited island, where he was
suckled by a wild roe, and grew up to manhood in a state
of utter isolation. Here, without any communication with
human beings, none of whom he had ever seen or spoken
to, "he attained," as Mr. Barclay declared, "to such a
profound knowledge of God, as to have immediate converse with Him, and to affirm that the *best and most certain*
knowledge of God 'was to be obtained by silent abstraction
from all material objects.' This abstraction he produced
by rapid evolutions of his body. Shutting his eyes, and
stopping his ears, he sustained a whirling motion until all
outward perception was temporarily withdrawn. In these
states of wrapt and silent ecstasy, Hai Eben, apart from
book or human teacher, attained, as was asserted, to a
profound knowledge of the highest truths, and especially
of such as are delivered in the Koran, which he had as yet
neither seen nor heard of. After spending fifty years on
his desert island, it was at length visited by a Moslem
stranger, with whom, after a time, he was able to converse, and from whom he received, orally, a detailed

account of the Mohammedan creed, its doctrines, and its paradise. "All which things," states the Arab historian, "Hai Eben Yokdan understood very well, and did not find any of them disagreeable to what he had seen when in that noble station; and he believed his visitor, and affirmed his veracity, and bore witness to his message."

It was not until many years after the death of the author of "The Apology," that it was discovered that what he had quoted as an authentic and actual history, was merely a romance, a sort of metaphysical Arabian "Robinson Crusoe," and that the astounding "fact" of Hai Eben's spiritual development by innate ideas, was one of the wildest conceptions of oriental fancy. Nevertheless, it had been received as authentic by very many, especially in America, and who were, by it, greatly confirmed in the dangerous opinions from which Hicksism sprang. This discovery of the fabulous nature of the story was not made till the republication of the Arabian work in all its details, after many editions of Barclay had issued. The official Friends, with characteristic prudence, forthwith ordered its suppression in future editions. The full title of the work is a lengthy and curious one, viz. :— "The improvement of human reason, exhibited in the Life of Hai Eben Yokdan; written in Arabic, above five hundred years ago, by Abu Jaafar Ebn Tophail; in which is demonstrated by what methods one may, by the mere light of nature, attain the knowledge of things natural and supernatural, more particularly the knowledge of God, and the affairs of another life. Newly translated from the original Arabic, by Simon Ockley, A.M., Vicar of Swavesey, in Cambridgeshire. London, printed, and

Dublin, reprinted, by and for Samuel Fuller, at the Globe
in Meath Street."

At a village in New England, Mr. Shillitoe exhibited
much vigour in protesting against a display of mischievous
Hicksite delusion in a Quaker lady, of otherwise virtuous
life and amiable manners, who had imbibed the notion
that outward ministry and Christian association were
unnecessary or undesirable for her. Having heard of the
miserable condition into which these visionary ideas had
reduced her, he obtained permission from her husband to
visit her, and found her immured in a close hot room, in
which, although it was warm American summer weather, she
had hung up pieces of woollen cloth over all crevices of
the door and windows, to exclude draughts. The poor
creature's countenance wore a dismal aspect, and she had
thus spent her time in chewing and moping for nearly two
years. Thomas, convinced that the wretched woman was
the victim of " a temptation of Satan," boldly told her as
much, and further called her " *a cumber-ground;*" for,
he adds, " if I spoke at all, it must be in plain terms."
This rousing and unceremonious style of address from a
stranger and a foreigner effected the desired purpose.
The delusion was dispelled, and the patient restored to her
right mind. She henceforth mingled with her friends,
attended public worship regularly, and again became a
useful and pleasant member of society.

Mr. Shillitoe held many meetings in the remote settle-
ments of the United States. At these he was much
disturbed by the squalling of the numerous infants brought
thither by their mothers who had no servants, or "helps,"
at home to take charge of them. Another practice which

much annoyed him, and against which he publicly protested, was the free-and-easy habit of bringing dogs into the meetings, where, during the attempted silence and preaching, they trotted about the room, or fought for the warmest places around the stove, and otherwise disturbed the quiet and solemnity of the gatherings. This appeared to be utterly without excuse, and Mr. Shillitoe accordingly made it the subject of exhortation and caution.

In America, as elsewhere, he visited the prisons, and some of the most influential persons in authority, including the President of the United States. Negroes and slave-owners also claimed his Christian solicitude. In Maryland he heard of a slave-merchant whose transactions in human flesh were of a very wholesale nature, and whose reputation for wickedness and ferocity indicated a character of the stamp of the infamous Legree, whom Mrs. Stowe has so graphically depicted in " Uncle Tom's Cabin." Mr. Shillitoe very naturally shrank from the prospect of visiting such a person. But duty pointed clearly, and, therefore, taking a companion, he proceeded to the residence of the merchant, not without much terror of the numerous savage dogs which were permitted to prowl around it unchained. The good man writes : " There was no way for me but to cast my care° on Him who had so many times preserved me as from the paw of the bear, and the jaws of the devourer." On approaching the mansion two of the large fierce dogs rushed toward the Friends, but, being observed by some house-slaves, were promptly called back. Presently the owner of the establishment made his appearance, roughly exclaiming, " What is your business ? " On explaining it courteously and mildly, he led them into an elegantly furnished room, and there afforded Mr. Shillitoe a full opportunity of earnestly pleading with him on behalf of the oppressed bondsmen. It was urged upon him that the proper way to attain a true conception of the matter was to place himself, his parents, his brothers and sisters, in imagination, in the condition of the slaves, and then to consider how far he could regard it as consistent with Christianity and obedience to God, to separate parent and child, husband and wife, and to enthral human beings, like brute beasts, in a bondage degrading alike to body and soul. The slave-owner was touched by the reference to his parents, and acknowledged that he had been brought up by a pious mother, who entertained such a rooted aversion to the slave system, as to induce her husband to liberate seventy slaves. After her death her young son had been surrounded by unfavourable influences, had entered the army of the United States, fought at New Orleans, and eventually entered into the slave traffic, in which he had acquired much wealth. But the remembrance of his pious mother, and his experience of the horrors and vices of the system, rendered him very much dissatisfied with it, and he had, at one period, made an attempt to abandon it, but was so strongly urged to continue it by acquaintances making a high profession as orthodox Christians, that, in the view of such strong religious sanction, he had maintained his establishment as before. But he now confessed that it was a bad business, and expressed a hope and belief that, in about twenty years, slavery would be extinct. He added that it was still his intention to quit his occupation at a suitable time. He then politely conducted his visitors through the array of chained and unchained dogs about the premises, and took a pleasant leave of them. Loaded pistols and other arms in various parts of his house indicated his sense of constant danger, and the necessity for vigorous precautions against insubordination or resistance. His courtesy to Mr. Shillitoe was the more remarkable, inasmuch as he had recently almost killed another Quaker, whom he had thrown down in the public streets and violently trampled on, for the offence of being an "abolitionist."

In a similar visit paid to another slave-owner, the absolute master of 300 bondsmen, Mr. Shillitoe's exhortations were not received so pleasantly, but merely elicited the acknowledgment, "Our views differ;" and a bold defence of the system, as being necessary for the discipline of an idle and improvident race, who were thus provided with physical care and religious instruction, of which they might, perhaps, otherwise be deprived.

After three years of arduous and often peculiarly painful labour in America, Mr. Shillitoe safely returned to England in the autumn of 1829. In his memoranda he says, "After a passage of twenty-eight days, I was released from the society of two as wicked men, cabin passengers, as I ever before had been in company with." On his arrival at Tottenham, he found his aged wife and his family all well, and rejoiced to welcome him back. In a thankful retrospect of his Transatlantic mission, he exclaims, "May I never forget the multiplied mercies of my Divine Care-taker, amidst the many perils and dangers to which I have been exposed; but, above all, that He was pleased to hear and answer my daily petitions to Him to preserve me out of the hands of men of unsound principles."

# CHAPTER VI.

## VISITS TO SOVEREIGNS AND INFLUENTIAL PERSONS.

PURELY RELIGIOUS SOURCE OF HIS VISITS TO SUCH PERSONS
—RECIPROCAL INFLUENCES OF RULERS AND SUBJECTS,
MINISTERS AND CONGREGATIONS, UPON EACH OTHER—IN-
DIVIDUAL RESPONSIBILITY—AS THE SEED, SO THE HARVEST
—VISIT TO THE PRESIDENT OF THE UNITED STATES—
WILLIAM CARTER'S UNION PRAYER MEETINGS—SCRIPTURAL
COMMANDS TO LABOUR FOR OTHERS IN PRAYER — MR.
SHILLITOE'S VISITS TO GEORGE THE THIRD AND GEORGE
THE FOURTH—HIS FAITHFUL COUNSEL TO THE LATTER—
INTERVIEWS WITH THE KINGS OF DENMARK AND PRUSSIA—
WILLIAM THE FOURTH AND QUEEN ADELAIDE—THE EM-
PEROR ALEXANDER OF RUSSIA—THE NINETY-FIRST PSALM
—ALEXANDER'S RELIGIOUS HISTORY— DANIEL WHEELER'S
ACCOUNT OF HIS LAST DAYS.

THE numerous interviews which Thomas Shillitoe was
in the habit of seeking with monarchs and persons in
authority did not originate in a love of notoriety, or a
mere morbid curiosity. They were, in general, services
from which he previously shrank with fear and much
reluctance, but which he persevered in from a sense of two
things—firstly, the power of influential men for good or
for evil; and, secondly, the responsibility of individuals
towards their authorities.

All history affords repeated examples of the blessed
influence and widely-efficient power of pious and godly

rulers, whether a Moses, a King Josiah, an Alfred the Great, or an Alexander the First. On the other hand, the demoralizing examples of a Charles the Second, a George the Fourth, or a Louis the Fifteenth, are similarly manifest. So, too, the influence of magistrates and clergymen gathers a special harvest either for God or for the devil. This truth is recognised in many a popular proverb, such as, "Like priest, like people." But it may also be reversed to "Like people, like priest," and "Like nation, like monarch;" for all influences are reciprocal.

A man in authority is only able to do good or evil in proportion to the circumstances of those he governs. If the latter are faithful and prayerful as individuals, their power is mighty to counteract official evil and to compel right action. Oftentimes rulers who have been the scourges of nations, such as, for instance, Robespierre, have felt and acknowledged that they were themselves urged onward by the spirit and character of the times, working out, as by the rushing of an irresistible mighty flood, the indispensable process of chastisement and discipline. When national evils have been long and persistently neglected by the great mass of individuals composing the nations, the measure of iniquity becomes full beyond the power of king or people to remove, and then some awful calamity is the certain and curative result, just as in some cases nothing avails to remedy a far-diseased limb, except the painful process of excision. Thus it was at the French Revolution. Courtly vice, and far worse still, priestly hypocrisy, had produced a nation of sceptics and profligates whose condition was so utterly corrupt,

that, in the virtual absence of the gospel and of a verna-
cular Bible, nothing could avail for correction but years of
awful discipline. The revolutionists and Napoleon arose
to administer that discipline.

So again, recently, in the United States. The plagues
of slavery had for a generation been increasing. They
had thoroughly corrupted the morals of every town and
village in the Southern States. Yet, blinded by self-
interest and deep-rooted prejudices, the pestilence was
nursed and fondled even by professing Christian churches,
and boldly patronized by ministerial and clerical conven-
tions. Then nothing further could be hoped for to stop
the inevitable crisis. Conflict and sword, terror and death,
were as sure to follow such national corruption as night
follows day. And so it resulted. The thunder-cloud
could not but burst. Five years of awful tribulation proclaimed to the slave supporters their inevitable responsibilities and punishment. Thus it always has been, and
thus it will continue, in every nation's experience as in
every individual's—" *Whatsoever* a man soweth, *that* shall
he also reap."

Thomas Shillitoe felt this truth deeply and abidingly.
Thus, when amongst Southern planters, he specially
defends his remonstrances addressed to them on the
ground of the apostolic precept, " Be not partaker of
other men's sins, but reprove them ;" a participation, he
adds, which is incurred unless individual efforts against
the offences, or in promotion of a remedy, are conscien-
tiously undertaken.

When visiting the President of the United States, at
Washington, in 1827, he said to that dignitary, " It has

long been my firm belief that, according to the power invested in us, so, if we do not exert that power and influence as far as in us lies, in preventing evil practices, we ourselves become implicated therein, in the sight of Almighty God, with those who are actually in the practice of them." He added, "It is my belief that if wickedness continues to increase in the United States as it has done, a scourge, in some way or another, will again be permitted to come upon the people."

In his labours for the Christian welfare of monarchs and authorities, Thomas Shillitoe acted on the principle so prominently set forth by the Apostle Paul in his epistle to Timothy—"I exhort, therefore, that, first of all, supplications, prayers, intercessions, and giving of thanks, be made for all men; for kings and for all that are in authority, *that we may live a quiet and peaceable life in all godliness and honesty.*"

He also recognized the same principle in its application to ministers of religion. But he does not appear to have urged the necessity of prayer for these so fully as their circumstances call for. Although the condition of congregations is greatly affected, for good or for evil, by the piety or carelessness of their ministers, yet, on the other hand, the zeal and efficiency of ministers are largely dependent upon the prayers and spiritual services of the individuals amongst whom they labour.

Thus at an interesting gathering at Stoke Newington, in February, 1867, Mr. William Carter, who has been very successful in home missions, especially in Southwark, gave a detailed account of the remarkable labours of himself and his coadjutors, and expressly traced their favourable results to two causes—firstly, to fervent, persevering, united prayer; and, secondly, to the plain and constant setting-forth of our Lord Jesus Christ as the Saviour of sinners, as the loving Son of God, bleeding and dying on the cross for men, and now risen on high, where He waits till He shall finally descend with His saints to establish His glorious everlasting kingdom, prophesied of so glowingly and abundantly in the pages of Holy Writ, especially in the Apocalypse and in the Prophets of the Old Testament.

Mr. Carter mentioned that he had given five thousand free teas to companies of thieves, prostitutes, and drunkards, who had been thus drawn within the sound of the gospel, and many of them permanently converted. They had given proofs of this by maintaining honest and virtuous behaviour in spite of severe temptations to the contrary. He had engaged for sabbath services, chiefly for these classes, the Victoria Theatre, the Deptford Dancing Rooms, and a hall at Kennington, for which latter alone he paid £150 per annum in rent, all or most of which was raised in voluntary contributions of pence by the poor attenders. Further, every Monday, he held Mothers' Meetings, at which six hundred women are taught to sew and work whilst improving books are read to them. Materials at wholesale prices are provided, and are purchased to the extent of £10 per week, all in coppers, which may be regarded as so much gin-money saved. These various mission efforts have resulted in abundant and abiding conversions. About two hundred persons have been thus led to devote themselves to the ministry of Christ's gospel, and some of them have gone to distant parts of the earth, even to Demerara and China, on mission services.

But all these successes have been evidently and peculiarly connected with the exercise of special and united prayer. On some occasions the Christian workers have come together for prayer, and have continued *all night* in supplication, from ten o'clock till six the next morning. And the results of such special prayer unions have been wonderful as to success in converting souls. Again, on some occasions the preacher has earnestly proclaimed the Gospel, but apparently with little result. Whereupon a band of Christian brothers and sisters have united for special prayer on his behalf, and the next evening his services have been attended by a marked and blessed success.

The work of conversion is God's. He will be acknowledged, and entreated, and leaned on in it. "Paul may plant, and Apollos water; but it is God who giveth the increase." This increase comes largely through prayer. It may seem mysterious that it should be so, but it is one of the plainest facts in church history. Many and many a time has it been with churches as it was with Israel in the wilderness. As long as Aaron and Hur held up Moses' hands in prayer, Israel prevailed; but when, through weariness, that prayer was relaxed, then Amalek prevailed. God blesses individual prayer, but collective prayer still more. The effects of the latter are often astonishing and unmistakeable. Much of the success of George Whitfield was owing to the encouragement derived through the united prayers of his friends and converts. It is said that in these union prayer-meetings he and

Wesley plumed their flight for the successful labours of their brilliant careers.

Our Lord proclaimed, when on earth, "The harvest truly is great, but the labourers are few. *Pray ye, therefore,* the Lord of the harvest, that he would send forth labourers into his harvest." Paul earnestly entreated the Roman Christians to pray for the success of his ministry. "I beseech you, brethren, for the Lord Jesus Christ's sake, and for the love of the Spirit, that ye *strive together* with me in your prayers to God for me, that I may be delivered from them that do not believe in Judea, and that my service which I have for Jerusalem may be accepted of the saints, that I may come unto you with joy by the will of God." Similarly to the Thessalonians he appealed: "Brethren, pray for us, that the word of the Lord may have free course and be glorified, even as it is with you, and that we may be delivered from unreasonable and wicked men."

In his Epistle to the Colossians, he takes particular notice of the service of prayer rendered by one of their own brethren. "Epaphras, who is one of you, a servant of Christ, saluteth you, always *labouring fervently for you in prayers*, that ye may stand perfect and complete in all the will of God."

The great High Priest and King of the universal Church, when on earth, showed forth the duty and example of *labouring* in prayer, "continuing all night in prayer," at times, and supplicating in the hour of urgent need, even "with strong crying and tears," even with the very sweat of blood.

Late years have witnessed almost unparallelled successes

in gospel labour, mainly by a revival of united prayer-meetings, especially in America, Ireland, and the metropolis. Such churches as have availed themselves of their use have profited exceedingly in consequence, and the word of God has been greatly multiplied.

Thomas Shillitoe, then, whilst deficient in his appreciation of union prayer-meetings, and even in his inculcation of individual responsibility in the matter of prayer for ministers, and for all persons exercising special influence upon others, yet practically exemplified in himself a sense of the value of intercessory prayer, and an obedient diligent solicitude for all in authority.

His first interview with royalty was in 1793, when, after a long and solemn impression of duty to address King George the Third, he proceeded to Windsor, and sought an opportunity of speaking to the monarch in the stable-yard, whither he generally came before his daily morning ride. Mr. Shillitoe and a companion, having ascertained that the King had come down to the stables, presented themselves there, but were being courteously repulsed by an attendant, when, his companion catching the King's eye, respectfully called out, " This friend of mine has something to communicate to the King." The latter at once walked towards the two Friends, followed by his attendants. He raised his hat and waited for Mr. Shillitoe to speak; but the latter kept silence for several minutes, whilst he prayerfully looked to the Lord for aid. He then, for about twenty minutes, earnestly addressed his sovereign in a very eloquent and heart-stirring discourse. Tears trickled down the cheeks of the royal old English gentleman, who then took a respectful leave of the two

Friends, and, instead of taking his ride, returned pensively to the Castle.

Previously to its accomplishment Mr. Shillitoe had been very anxious in view of this service, and a few minutes before the address, he says, he felt " not only like a vessel emptied of anything it ever contained to communicate of a religious nature to others, but, as it were, washed from the very dregs." Immediately he had spoken the first words of his discourse, " Hear, O King!" all fear left him, and he stood like a wall of brass. And after having completely discharged the duty, he says, "his relief was comparable to that felt by a porter who has got rid of a heavy burden which had been long crushing him down.

His next interview with royalty was with the Prince Regent, at Brighton, in 1813. As it appeared quite unlikely that a full opportunity would be afforded for verbally communicating all that, on this occasion, Mr. Shillitoe believed he was called upon to deliver, he previously embodied his feelings in a written address, which he now desired to place in the hands of the Prince, and personally to invite his perusal of it. This time, too, it seemed most probable that the best opportunity of presentation would be afforded, by watching for the Prince's appearance in commencing his usual ride on the Downs. Accordingly, Mr. Shillitoe and three Friends posted themselves outside the palace-gate, towards the Downs, till the Prince should pass them. At length, the latter, with a numerous retinue, rode out, but, to the disappointment of the good men, turned away in the opposite direction from his usual route. Mr. Shillitoe seeing this, and feeling that he must seize the opportunity, set off at a rapid run after the Prince, but was out of breath when he came abreast of him, and, therefore, proceeded some way further to secure a brief rest; and as soon as the Prince was again opposite to him, he called out, " Will the Prince be pleased to permit me to express a few words to him? " On which, the latter checked his horse, stooped forward, and replied, " Sir, you must excuse me; I am in haste." Mr. Shillitoe persevered, saying, he had a letter for him, might it be received? The Regent replied, " You will please give it to Colonel Bloomfield." Mr. Shillitoe then delivered it to that attendant, and succeeded in obtaining from him a promise that it should really be placed in the Prince's hands. There is reason to believe that this was done, and that the letter produced some impression. On the following day a magnificent banquet had been announced, to celebrate the birthday of one of the royal family; but, suddenly and without any explanation, the court visitors were disappointed by its being countermanded. And, after an interval of eleven years, when Mr. Shillitoe had another interview with the Prince, then George the Fourth (at Windsor, in 1824), he reminded the King that he had previously presented him with an address, at Brighton. The latter responded, " I remember you did."

Probably, no noble or prelate ever ventured to address such plain-spoken and yet kindly words to the debauched and effeminate Prince, as the humble Quaker had penned in that letter taken to him at Brighton. It was a faithful and bold service to set before the royal profligate the earnest pleadings of which the following are the chief passages :—

" I have endeavoured, as far as possible, to place myself, mentally, in thy exposed situation, and it is with real sympathy that I entreat thee to suffer the word of exhortation.  Our being prone to sin by nature will not be charged against us in the great day when our future eternal situation shall be decided, if in good earnest we have been endeavouring, through Divine assistance, to overcome the evil propensities of our fallen nature; the sin is not in being tempted, but in yielding to temptation; and suffer me to say, that if thou hadst accepted and co-operated with the offers of Divine Grace, and the all-efficient help inwardly manifested, there would be no grounds for *those remarks upon thy intemperance*, which, of late years, have been so generally made, but which, I earnestly hope, have been greatly exaggerated.

" Many of those who hang about princes for their own interested purposes, are strewing with flowers the path which leads to the edge of a precipice, and are sedulously employed in concealing that horrid precipice from view. Such are real enemies.

" Words fail me to set forth the conflict of mind, which at times I have passed through for many years, on account of thy precious immortal soul, O Prince !  For although, as an earthly Prince, thou art invested with great power, and art made ruler and head of a mighty nation, thou rankest no higher, in the Divine estimation, *than the lowest of thy subjects*, further than as thou art found walking with God in obedience to His revealed will, and righteously filling up the very awful and important station which, by Divine permission, thou art standing in.  So great has been the anguish and affliction of soul which I have experienced on thy account, and so strong the desires which I have felt for thy everlasting welfare, that I have thought, if the offering up of my natural life as a sacrifice would have effected it, I could have felt willing. But I am deeply and consolingly convinced, that no man can save his brother, or give to God a ransom for the soul of his friend, yet, through infinite mercy, a ransom has been paid by the One Propitiatory Sacrifice for sin. But to obtain an evidence of our interest in this Sacrifice, we must be willing to receive Christ in His inward and spiritual appearance in the heart, where He would put an end to sin, finish transgression, and bring in everlasting righteousness. For the great and awful work of salvation, if it is ever known to be accomplished, *must become an individual work;* and that this important business may no longer be deferred by thee, all that is within me, capable of feeling, craves at this time, under an awful sense, which has long accompanied my mind, of the extreme danger thou art in from further procrastination.

" I believe, never has the report gone abroad and reached my ear of thy grand entertainments being about to take place, but my poor mind has felt sorrow on thy account ; and in spirit I have been with thee as a mournful spectator at the banquet. I have contemplated thee as surrounded by those whom thou callest thy friends ; but what if they should prove in the end thy greatest enemies ? for, Prince as thou art, thou must appear before the tribunal of Divine justice and judgment. How wilt thou then give an account of these scenes of dissipation ? *Remember the decrees of the Great Judge are unalterable ; and against them there lies no appeal.* It will not avail thee then to plead that thou wast countenanced in these things, by those for whose age and experience, and even religious knowledge, thou hadst respect. The awful determination will surely be accomplished, *According to thy works so shall thy reward be.*

"And what is the greatest amongst men when left to himself and bereft of the assistance of his Maker? When laid upon a death-bed, what can the prayers of others avail thee, if He who alone can save—He whose offers of help in time of health have been slighted, then refuses to hear? Just and equal are the ways of the Lord, If we suffer the day of our visitation to pass over unimproved, the determination will stand, 'When they call I will not answer.'

"With fervent desires for thy real happiness, both here and hereafter, I remain, dutifully and very respectfully,

"Thy sincere Friend,

"THOMAS SHILLITOE."

The Prince Regent might well say, "I remember," in reference to such a truly loyal and nobly Christian appeal, as the above. But probably he had already well-nigh become finally reprobate and hopelessly hardened. For surely, if not, he must have been solemnized and awakened by the affecting evidence which the poor old monarch, his father, presented of the nothingness, even of royalty, to save itself in the hour of trial. Upon him, in his age, the double darkness of madness and blindness had come down, and until death his lot was to be one of the saddest possible:—

"Total eclipse! no sun, no moon,
All dark, amid the blaze of noon."

It was in April, 1824, that Mr. Shillitoe (accompanied by his congenial and excellent friend, Peter Bedford) again met George the Fourth. This time it was in the

Long Walk, at Windsor, where the King was driving his pony-chaise. On being approached by the two Friends, he stopped his horses, and not only gave Mr. Shillitoe permission to hand him a memorial, but also stayed to listen to a few earnest words which the good man addressed to him. After which the King replied, " I thank you." The memorial, unlike the one at Brighton, contained scarcely any reference to the King's own religious condition, but was exclusively directed towards calling his attention to the sabbath desecration and open immorality prevalent in the royal dominions in Hanover, which Mr. Shillitoe had recently visited.

No further communications appear to have passed between him and George the Fourth. But it has been said, that when that monarch was on his death-bed, he called out " Oh! that Quaker, that Quaker!" probably as if oppressed with a deep sense of despair and remorse at his inattention to the counsels which his faithful and godly subject had long ago urged upon his attention.

When at Copenhagen, in 1821, Mr. Shillitoe had a series of very satisfactory interviews with the King and Queen of Denmark, also with the princesses, the prime minister, and members of the cabinet council. The King afterwards sent him a message, expressing a desire that some English Friends might come and settle in his dominions, offering them a large tract of land in Jutland, and promising them his special protection, and his royal respect for their peculiar scruples of conscience, as, for instance, against bearing arms. But it does not appear that this kind offer induced any of Mr. Shilitoe's community to emigrate to Denmark.

At Berlin, in 1824, Mr. Shillitoe visited the Crown Prince of Prussia, by whom he was very pleasantly received. His address was listened to with deep attention, and at its termination, the Prince, taking hold of his visitor's hands, exclaimed, " Do not forget me, Do not forget me !" A few days afterwards, the King of Prussia accorded an interview to Mr. Shillitoe in the palace-gardens of Charlottenburg. After having spoken a short time, the King, who had taken off his cap, exclaimed to his prime minister who was in attendance, " I see what he wants—Sunday to be well observed. Tell him I have read his address to Hamburg, and it has pleased me much ;" adding, " I wish the Lord may bless you in these your undertakings." The Friend then continued his remarks, and spoke of other public matters which called for alteration ; on which the King replied, " I am one with you in this respect, but it requires time ; such disorders are not easily remedied." Mr. Shillitoe then added, that it was his firm belief, that " by the King's thus endeavouring to do all in his power towards promoting true religion and righteousness amongst his subjects, it would do more towards his being preserved in a peaceable and quiet possession of his dominions, than all the fortifications or armies he could possibly raise." The King responded, " I believe so myself."

After some further observations on both sides the interview terminated pleasantly, and the King ordered an attendant to show Mr. Shillitoe over his palace and gardens, and, in particular, to conduct him to the new mausoleum of his late beloved Queen.

In 1832 (at the age of 78) he was permitted a free opportunity of expressing the feelings of his mind on various important matters to King William the Fourth and Queen Adelaide, who, in separate interviews at Windsor Castle, received him very pleasantly, and entered familiarly into conversation on various points. King William did not evince a very accurate acquaintance with the history and constitution of his Quaker subjects, inasmuch as he appeared to think they were identical with the Moravians or Herrnhuters, and supposed that William Penn was the founder of the sect. Mr. Shillitoe and his companion Peter Bedford corrected these misapprehensions, and the former, continuing his address, spoke of his frequent earnest prayers for the King. "that the Almighty would be pleased to incline his heart so to walk in the ways of His requirings, that he might become a blessing to the nation over whom he is permitted to reign, and that the Lord may incline the heart of the King, to seek daily for help to be enabled to maintain the noble resolution of one formerly,—' Let others do as they may, I will serve the Lord ; ' and then, when called upon to surrender up his earthly crown, that he might be favoured to receive the crown designed for him to wear in the kingdom of Heaven."

In visiting Queen Adelaide Mr. Shillitoe acknowledged her kindly sympathies for the poorest classes of her subjects, entreated her continued solicitude for these, and besought her to use her influence in discouraging the use of machine-made fabrics, stating his belief that the introduction of machinery was doing much mischief to the country, and throwing many poor persons out of employ, adding that it was " allowed on all sides that goods manufactured by hand were generally much more serviceable

than those made by machinery." His companion, Peter
Bedford (himself a Spitalfields silk-manufacturer), then
took up the subject, and informed the Queen that her
patronage of English-made silk had already been of much
service. Mr. Shillitoe records, " The satisfaction that
gleamed in the countenance of the Queen at this informa-
tion was very striking.

The two good aged men were more at home in religious
matters than on questions of political economy and machine-
labour. It was very natural, however, that, in a matter
wherein the occupation of one of them was concerned, they
should look at it from a one-sided and partial point of
view. It was also to be expected that persons far advanced in age should be old-fashioned in their notions.
Mr. Shillitoe concluded his visit to the Queen by a solemn
and appropriate religious discourse.

The two visits which Mr. Shillitoe paid to the Emperor
Alexander the First of Russia (at Petersburg, in 1824)
were probably the most interesting of all his interviews
with eminent persons. When first introduced to the
Emperor, the latter commenced by enquiring, with deep
interest, after the two Quaker missionaries, Stephen
Grellet and William Allen, with whom he had previously
been on very intimate terms of Christian communion.
Then ensued a free and open discourse on a variety of
subjects connected with the religious and moral welfare of
the Russian empire and of its head. The Quaker and the
Emperor then (at the particular request of the latter)
spent some time together in united but silent prayer ; and,
at the close of the interview, the Emperor thus freely
expressed himself to his humble but pious visitant :—

" Before I became acquainted with your religious Society and its principles, I frequently, from my early life, felt something in myself which at times gave me clearly to see that I stood in need of a further knowledge of Divine things than I was then in possession of; which I could not then account for, nor did I know where to look for that which would prove availing to my help in this matter, until I became acquainted with some of your Society and with its principles. This I have since considered to be the greatest of all the outward blessings the Almighty has bestowed upon me ; because hereby I became fully satisfied in my own mind, that that which had thus followed me, though I was ignorant of what it meant, was that same Divine power, inwardly revealed, which your religious Society have, from their commencement, professed to be actuated by in their daily walks through life ; whereby my attention became turned with increased earnestness to seek after more of an acquaintance with it in my own soul. And I bless the Lord that He thus continues to condescend to send His true gospel ministers to keep me in remembrance of this day of His merciful awakening to my soul."

He then added, " My mind is at times brought under great suffering to know how to move along. I see things necessary for me to do, and things necessary for me to refuse complying with, which are expected from me. You have counselled me to an unreserved and well-timed obedience in all things. I clearly see it to be my duty ; and this is what I want to be more brought into the experience of. But, when I try for it, doubts come into my mind, and discouragements prevail. For, although they call me an absolute monarch, *it is but little power I have*, for doing that which I see it to be right for me to do."

On Mr. Shillitoe rising to take leave, the Emperor grasping him by the hand, said, with deep interest, " I, shall not consider this as a parting opportunity, but shall expect another visit from you before you set off for your own home." Mr. Shillitoe remarks, " I observed the Emperor turned himself from me, as I fully believe in order to give vent to his tears of gratitude to that Almighty Power who in mercy had been pleased to favour us together with the precious overshadowing influence of His good presence ; an evidence of which I never remember to have been more sensible of."

At his second visit to the Emperor, Mr. Shillitoe called his attention, in particular, to the depraved condition of a multitude of serfs in Russia, to the filthy and neglected condition of the prisoners, to the cruel infliction of the knout, and to the discouragement and almost cessation of the operations of the Bible Society in Petersburg, owing, in great degree, to the opposition of the Greek Metropolitan in that city. He concluded his address with the words, " Seeing things are thus managed, may I not add the language of the Most High, through one of His prophets, ' Shall I not visit for these things ? ' "

Then, after a period of solemn silence, he knelt down and prayed earnestly, the Emperor also kneeling at his side. After which, on taking his final leave, he records, " The time for my departure being come, I rose to go, and, after holding each other affectionately by the hand, he saluted me, and we took a heart-tendering farewell."

Whilst in Petersburg he also had two very satisfactory

visits to the pious Prince Alexander Galitzin, the prime minister. This dignitary, who had been brought up from childhood with the Emperor Alexander, had exercised a most valuable influence upon the latter. He it was who first induced Alexander to read the Holy Scriptures. This was about the year 1812, when the extraordinary and providential circumstances connected with the deliverance of Russia from the hands of Napoleon and his vast hosts, roused the attention of many in that empire to serious things. At the time when Napoleon entered Moscow, a general panic seized the inhabitants of Petersburg lest he should march thither also. Accordingly, multitudes prepared to flee, and the Emperor also contemplated removal from his palace. Prince Alexander Galitzin, however, continuing calm and unmoved amid the turmoil, excited the suspicion of enemies, who reported to the Emperor that he must be secretly in league with Napoleon. On this the Emperor visited him, and expressed his surprise at his undisturbed demeanour. The Prince replied that he was indeed confident and calm. " Whence have you such confidence ? " enquired the Emperor. He replied, " I feel it in my heart, and it is also stated in this divinely-inspired volume." He then handed a Bible to the Emperor, but it fell from his grasp to the floor and opened. The Prince, glancing at its pages, saw that it opened at the 91st Psalm: " He that dwelleth in the secret place of the tabernacle of the Most High shall abide under the shadow of the Almighty. I will say of the Lord, He is my refuge and my fortress; my God, in Him will I trust. He shall cover thee with His feathers, and under His wings shalt thou trust. His truth shall be thy shield and buckler. A thousand shall fall at thy side, and ten thousand at thy right hand, but it shall not come nigh thee." He read these words to the Emperor, who was much impressed by them. The latter presently prepared to quit the city, but first entered the cathedral for a farewell service. To his astonishment a priest read aloud the 91st Psalm. On the Emperor sending to ask him why he read that portion, he replied that he had prayed the Lord to direct him to such portion of Scripture as might be most suitable under the Emperor's peculiar circumstances, and that psalm had been brought before his attention. Late that evening, in his palace, the Emperor desired an attendant to read to him out of the Bible. Once more he was astounded to hear the 91st Psalm. He at once exclaimed, " Who told you to read this? Has Galitzin told you ? " The attendant said he had neither seen Prince Galitzin nor had any one spoken to him on the subject ; but that, having prayed to God to guide him in reading, he had chosen that psalm. The Emperor, after this threefold indication of its being a divine message for his comfort and encouragement, became increasingly serious, and henceforth read in private a chapter of the Bible every morning and evening, and meditated on the same.

These particulars were communicated to Messrs. Grellet and Allen by the Prince. The Emperor himself related to them other incidents of his previous life, mentioning that, when a child, he had been placed by his grandmother, the Empress Catharine, under the care of talented but sceptical tutors. He was, however, also trained in the observances of the Greek Church, and was taught to repeat a regular form of prayer morning and evening, but he disliked this practice. But on several occasions, after retiring to rest, he had experienced solemnizing Divine visitations of his soul, which so tendered him that he had arisen from bed and prayed on his knees, with tears, that the Lord would forgive his sins, and strengthen him to act rightly. As years passed over him and he entered more into the pleasures of the Court, those serious impressions became almost effaced. But in 1812, the flames of Moscow and the influence of the good Prince Galitzin, again recalled him to the fear and service of God. Then, too, he read the Bible, for the first time, with real interest. " I devoured it," he said, " finding in it words so suitable to, and descriptive of, the state of my mind. The Lord, by His Divine Spirit, was also pleased to give me an understanding of what I read therein."

At the solemn religious interviews which Stephen Grellet* and William Allen had with the Emperor (in 1819), they united both in silent worship and in fervent vocal prayer. The Emperor was so much affected that, Mr. Grellet records—" He was bathed in tears."

Mr. Shillitoe's interviews with Alexander were in 1824. Next year, the good Emperor died.

That event is thus alluded to in a letter (dated Petersburg, December 13, 1825,) from Daniel Wheeler :— " When the intelligence of the Emperor's death was made

---

* For the particulars of the deeply interesting biography of Stephen Grellet, " the apostle of modern Quaker Missions," see his Life, in two volumes, by B. Seebohm: F. B. Kitto (5, Bishopsgate Street Without, London). For a shorter account of Grellet, see also, five papers in the "Sunday at Home " for 1866, by the writer of this book.

public in the city, general consternation soon spread to all ranks of the people.   At first I thought it possible there might be some mistake, as the health of the Empress Elizabeth* had been for some time declining, which occasioned her journey to the South of Russia.   But the military being called upon to swear allegiance to the new Emperor Constantine, removed every doubt.

" I only felt one desire.   This was, that the death of Alexander might have been a fair one.   And we have the most indisputable proof that it has been unattended with any of those horrid circumstances which have so often terminated the existence of the crowned heads of this country.   I have often put up a petition that the hand of violence might never be permitted to touch him ; and, although I cannot help deploring, with the many thousands of Russia, the loss of such a man, yet a secret joy triumphs over every selfish feeling, and raises in my heart a tribute of gratitude and thankfulness to the great Preserver of men, who hath been graciously pleased to remove him from this scene of conflict, trouble and dismay.

" I believe it has been the lot of but few monarchs to end their days whilst in the meridian of power, in a retreat so quiet and so distant from all the pageantry of a court.† It may be said he died in the bosom of his family.   For

---

* With whom, also, Mr. Shillitoe had had two very satisfactory interviews.   She was a truly humble and heartily pious Christian, and died a few months after the decease of the Emperor.

† Alexander died at Taganrog, in the far south of Russia, not without strong suspicion of being poisoned.   But this suspicion appears to have been unfounded.

the first two or three days of his indisposition, it appears that he considered it of no importance, and could not be prevailed upon to take any medicine, to which he had an aversion at all times. The climate around Taganrog is considered very healthy, but at a very short distance from it it is quite the reverse. It seems that Alexander had been beyond the healthy boundary, and had taken cold upon the south coast.

" It is very consoling to find that his mind was so peaceful, as appears to have been the case, when he was persuaded to take the sacrament. It is probable that delirium came on afterwards; but towards the last he was perfectly sensible and collected.

" On the morning he died, the sun broke through the clouds and shone into the room, when he said,—' How beautiful the weather is!' And the manner in which he committed the Empress to the care of Prince Volkousky, his faithful adjutant, although done without the assistance of words, plainly shows that he was collected, though deprived of speech.

" From concurring circumstances, of late date, my hope is greatly strengthened that he has exchanged an earthly crown for one immortal, that will never fade away. He had reigned about four months less than twenty-five years. The Russians say he was too mild and too good for them."

Space would fail to enter into all the particulars of Mr. Shillitoe's various visits to queens, nobles, archbishops, bishops and magistrates. Suffice it to say that all were undertaken from similar motives of earnest desire to serve God and to promote righteousness among men.

# CHAPTER VII.

## EFFORTS IN PROMOTION OF TEMPERANCE.

INTEMPERANCE CHIEFLY EVIL BECAUSE OF ITS ANTAGONISM TO RELIGIOUS EFFORT—TESTIMONIES OF EXPERIENCED PERSONS—MR. SHILLITOE'S LABOURS IN THE WHISKY-SHOPS OF WATERFORD, CORK, &C.—INSULTS RECEIVED—ARDUOUS VISITATION OF SIX HUNDRED DRINKING-HOUSES IN DUBLIN —SCENE IN A CELLAR—HIS OWN REMARKABLE EXPERIENCES OF STIMULANTS AND ABSTINENCE—HIS EXTREME NERVOUSNESS MUCH LESSENED—DR. CHANNING ON THE MORAL EVILS AND IMPERCEPTIBLE APPROACH OF INTEMPERANCE.

MR. SHILLITOE's early acquaintance with public-house life probably tended to rouse his attention to the enormous evils of intemperance. But whether this was the case or not, it became evident to him, very early in his ministerial career, that religious labour was, in numerous cases, of little or no avail so long as its objects indulged in intemperate habits. Many years before the question was taken up actively, even by its first pioneers, and whilst even his brother Quakers were, in general, indifferent, if not actually opposed, to such efforts, he entered actively into an arduous and life-long combat with the master-evil drunkenness. For experience and observation had practically led him to the conclusions arrived at half-a-century later by the bulk of philanthropic and enlightened men. But, before entering on a review of his labours on the question, it may be well to adduce a few of the more recent testimonies respecting it, for the interest of readers not as yet impressed by the urgency of this question.

Archdeacon Garbett (speaking of beer-shops, &c.) says : " I have seen schools excellently managed, the most regular cottage visiting, *the most heart-searching preaching*, *all*, so far as the labourer and cottager are concerned, *thrown away* on this rock." For religious instruction needs a suitable soil ; just as the best seed is sown in vain on undrained or untilled land.

Lord Shaftesbury declared :—" From my own knowledge and experience as a Commisioner of Lunacy for the last twenty years, and as Chairman of the Commission during sixteen years, fortified by enquiries in America, I find that *fully six-tenths of all the cases of insanity* to be found in these realms, and in America, arise from no other cause than from habits of intemperance."

The Rev. John Clay, Chaplain of Preston Gaol, stated his belief, after long and accurate observation, that *nine-tenths* of English crime arises from intemperance ; and further states, " I would note the fact, that during *two* years, I have heard 1126 prisoners attribute their offences— frauds, larcenies, robberies, burglaries, rapes, stabbing, homicides—to drink ! "

The late Bishop of Bath and Wells (Dr. G. H. Law,) said,—" Often have I noticed that in those parishes where there was not a single public-house, there the greatest regularity and happiness were to be found ; but in the *direct ratio* of public-houses was the increase of vice and misery."

Mrs. Sewell, in her ballad " The Rose of Cheriton,"* has put into the mouth of a working man, in homely rhyme, a common-sense view of the urgent needs of his class in reference to drinking temptations :—

> " We want help to struggle from the slough
> Placed in the way of working-people now.
> We want the workman's interest to stand
> Before the licensed victuallers of the land.
> We want a law, sir, that should put away
> The accursed drinking on the Sabbath-day.
> And workmen want the power to prevent,
> Or rather, sir, they want that Parliament
> Should use its noblest power to legislate,
> And neither give excise nor magistrate
> All but unbridled liberty to grant
> A public pest that workmen *do not want*,—
> The beer-shop, which all sober people hate
> Close to their home, close to their garden gate,
> Where the young child, upon its mother's breast,
> May learn the language of the drunkard's nest,
> And see its outcome, that in little time
> Is sentenced by the magistrate, as crime.
> With law expense—expenses more and more,
> For prosecuting the degraded poor !"
>
>      *      *      *      *      *
>
> " But, still," I said, " good friend, you must confess
> A man's not saved, though cured of drunkenness;
> He has a deeper root of sin within
> That's not destroyed, although he drink no gin.
> There must be faith, a living faith, you know,
> On which the fruits of righteousness must grow."
>
> " True, sir, most true, but the Apostle Paul
> Said 'faith' must come by 'hearing' if at all.
> But through what channel shall the drinker hear ?
> Parsons don't preach where men are tippling beer.

* London : S. W. Partridge, 9, Paternoster Row.   Price 6d.

And therefore do we strive, and strive again,
To break, if possible, his heavy chain;
That he may quit the pothouse for the pew,
And hear of faith, and hope, and mercy, too;
May hear of Jesus, and of sin forgiven,
And seek henceforward holiness and heaven."

Mainly from its deadly antagonism to Christianity, and to the progress of Christ's work in the hearts of individuals, and in the morals of communities, Mr. Shillitoe opposed intemperance to the utmost. His labour in that direction was entered upon as being a most legitimate and important function of his Christian mininistry.

It was during his first visit to Ireland, in 1808, that he first entered heartily into the work of combating intemperance, and from that period till his death, in 1836, he vigorously continued the contest. During that Irish journey he commenced his religious temperance campaign by paying ninety-three visits to the whisky-shops in and around the city of Waterford. Crowds of people followed him and his companion from house to house; the market-women cursed them, others joked and jibed; but the Friends quietly persevered in their arduous course of kindly exhortation and Christian protest.

They next paid similar visits to several score drinking-houses in and around Carrick-on-Suir. Here they did not meet with much active opposition, but were "a gazing stock," and were abused as "antichrist."

The drinking-shops of New Ross next claimed their attention and visitation.

In 1810 Mr. Shillitoe started on a second Irish journey. He now visited the whisky-shops of Clonmel, taking them at the rate of thirty a-day. Then followed forty similar visits at Kilkenny, and twenty more at Callan.

In 1811, during a third journey to Ireland, he undertook the disagreeable service of visiting the very numerous drinking-houses in the larger cities.

At Cork he paid several hundred visits of this nature, and here he met with some very violent opposition. Some girls " set upon us as if they intended to do us a mischief, calling us two devils ; saying, if it was not for our respectable appearance, they would beat our heads flat with a pot." At another place, a number of rude women followed the Friends into a drinking-house, dancing and screaming out for whisky. But some appreciated their devoted zeal, and exclaimed, " Our priest does not give such proof of his care for our welfare." One intelligent and civil whisky-seller said to them, " Go, speak to the Government ; for if your mission does not extend beyond this, it is doing but little. I wish all the world were Quakers, for I believe them to be the nearest to the truth of any sect ; but money has done that for them which persecution could not. By their seeking after money they are very much become like other people again." Some ran away from them, others insulted, and not a few listened attentively. At one place, Mr. Shillitoe mentions that " a big, dirty-looking man, who was taking his pint of beer at the bar, after filling his mouth with the beer, squirted it in my face and bosom, telling me to take that for Jesus Christ's sake, declaring he would go for the poker, and left us as if he was determined to put his threats in practice. But his threats did not discourage me, feeling the assurance he would not be permitted to hurt a hair of my head. I was mercifully preserved in the quiet, and we saw no more of him." Many of these Cork houses were exceedingly filthy, and reeking with intolerable fumes and odours.

He next proceeded to Watergrass Hill, Rathcormack, and Furmagh. At the latter place alone he made sixty visits, receiving, as usual, very various receptions. One man replied to his address, that " No alms-deeds, no good works, no sacrifices, no Jew, no Turk, no religion, could enter the kingdom : none but Roman Catholics could be admitted." At another house dirty water was showered upon him. Elsewhere, a man threatened him with a large butcher's knife.

The arduous undertaking of visiting the whisky-shops of Limerick was next entered on. Here they were abused as " false prophets and false teachers."

Clogheen, Cahir, and other places, were then similarly visited. At these and other places, Mr. Shillitoe called upon the priests, and set before them the very dangerous reliance of the masses of the people on the presumed power of priestly absolution, thinking that they might from time to time get drunk and otherwise sin, with impunity, after each successive grant of such priestly pardon. But he urged that this would not avail at the Divine Tribunal. It would only redound to deeper condemnation.

He now went to Dublin, and though his soul revolted from the very idea of personally labouring in its multitudinous whisky-dens and haunts of low vice, the duty seemed plain and imperative. Humbly, and in much prayerful dependence on the Lord, he proceeded to obey.

But what a labour, indeed, it was. *Six hundred* of

these houses, for the most part filthy, low-ceiled, close, and noisy, were visited by this devoted Christian minister, in Dublin alone! Day after day, for more than seven weeks, did he pursue his extraordinarily difficult undertaking. Several times he had to give over for the day, after performing some half-a-dozen visits, as nature was exhausted. At other times he proceeded most undauntedly, and on one occasion performed thirty-five visits in the day. Of course his reception comprehended all manner of treatment. One young man gratefully acknowledged his efforts as being those of a father of the people. "At one place it appeared as if the whole neighbourhood was set in battle-array against us." Elsewhere, he was asked if he was ordained. Then, being in vain offered first beer, and next spirits, a man called for bacon, declaring he would see what his visitor was, and whether he would eat swine's flesh or not. A landlord, pale with rage, said, "as I would eat meat on a Friday, I was going the high-road to hell. He wished he had us out, declaring what he would do to us." At another place, a man justified drunkenness, on the ground that the apostle Paul had pledged his cloak for wine, aad so had to leave it at Troas, but he afterwards repented. He added, that St. Patrick also permitted Catholics to get drunk in his honour, as his saint's day. Hence, there could be no harm in it on other occasions.

In Barrack Street, on descending a drinking-cellar, Mr. Shillitoe witnessed a wretched scene. In a large room were parties of men and women drinking. Young girls lay on the benches, utterly exhausted with the night's revelry, and drunk to insensibility. Others were dancing without shoes, stockings, or caps. A fiddler was tuning up merrily. The windows were smashed, and even their frames broken. For some time after Mr. Shillitoe attempted to address the woman in charge of this den, the dancers continued whirling round him, and the fiddle drowned his voice. But at length the earnestness and seriousness of the Friends commanded attention. The music and dancing ceased, and the wretched revellers listened to what was declared to them. Mr. Shillitoe thus describes the conclusion of this particular visit :—" After strength was received to utter that which was given me, and I had been some time engaged in addressing this band of human misery, I think I shall not, whilst I am favoured with my mental powers, wholly lose sight of the distress and horror portrayed in the countenances of those young women who had ceased their dancing to the fiddle. Feeling my mind relieved, and being about to depart, such of the company as were equal to it rose from their seats, acknowledging their gratitude for the labour that had been extended, and their desire that what had been offered might not be lost upon them, and that a blessing might attend us."

Our space precludes us from describing the other similar services rendered simultaneously to the promotion of religion and of temperance by Mr. Shillitoe.

But some reference must be made to his own personal experience.

He was subject throughout life to visitations of very severe nervous depression and anxiety, alternating at other times with much cheerfulness. On some occasions he suffered so acutely from hypochondriacal attacks as to

K

be brought almost to the verge of death.    Thus, in 1805, he records that his state of body and mind was such "a pit of horrors," that he thought he should sink under it. On other occasions his feelings were so morbid that he would fancy himself a teapot for weeks together, and be in dread when persons came close to him, lest they should break him.    He has been known to run whilst crossing London Bridge, from fear that it might give way under him.    After the occurrence of a very terrible murder, which had excited general horror, he kept indoors for a considerable time, from a dread that he might be mistaken for the murderer, and treated accordingly.    He records in one of his memoranda, "Twice I was confined to my bed from the sudden sight of a mouse."

For these ailments he tried many prescriptions, and especially stimulants, but without success.    At length he entered on a contrary course, and confined himself to a most rigid diet of entire abstinence from all intoxicating beverages and from animal food (except milk and eggs). The result was very satisfactory, inasmuch as, for the last thirty years of his life, his health and strength were greatly superior to that of earlier years.    During the whole period of his Irish, Continental, and American travel, he was a total abstainer from alcohol and flesh.

He was, however, more or less nervous to the end of life, though not nearly to the extent felt in former years.    Thus, when the postman brought letters to his door, Mr. Shillitoe on receiving them would frequently place them unopened in a cupboard or drawer.    He would then walk about his garden for some time in much anxiety and nervous dread, lest there should be some alarming or unpleasant tidings in the letters. Then, finally, he would screw up his courage to open and read them.

In May, 1833 (at the age of 79) he walked from Tottenham to Exeter Hall to address a temperance meeting. In that speech, he detailed the circumstances of his experience on the question, and stated that for twenty years, from the twenty-fourth year of his age, he had, in obedience to medical orders, habitually taken a generous diet of beefsteak and good ale for breakfast, and a liberal supply of wine and ale at dinner and supper. With all this support his nerves became weaker and his health deteriorated. Debility and frequent " horrors " were his usual condition. He was then advised to smoke and to take spirits and water. But, now in addition to the previous ailments, he began to lose his sleep. Laudanum was therefore prescribed. He began with ten drops a day, and found it necessary to increase the dose by three drops every third night. This plan was adopted until his nightly portion was *one hundred and eighty drops.* Notwithstanding all this vigorous and persevering obedience to medical orders, his health did not improve. To use his own words, " I became bilious, rheumatic, and gouty. I frequently had very bad colds and sore throat, and I can only describe the situation I was brought into, by saying I went about day by day frightened for fear of being frightened—a dreadful situation indeed to be living in."

He next consulted a medical friend in Hampshire, who recommended him to abandon stimulants ; but about the same time his London physician ordered him to double his ale, and, in particular, to drink very old Madeira wine. The patient accordingly procured some of the latter twenty years old; but he had become so weak, that even this had little more effect upon him than so much water.

After having thus almost boxed the compass of medical advice and of stimulant experience, he resolved to try complete abstinence from everything intoxicating; but this he felt would be a work of such extreme difficulty, that only fervent persevering prayer for God's help could obtain him the needful strength. He says, "I made up my mind to seek for help from Almighty God, satisfied as I was, *that nothing short of His help* could enable me to endure the conflict I must undergo. Favoured, as I believe I was, with that holy help that would bear me up in making the attempt, I proceeded *all at once (for I found tampering with these things would not do)* and gave up my laudanum, fermented liquors of every kind whatsoever, and my meat breakfast. My health has gradually improved from that time to the present; so that I am able to say, to the praise of Him who enabled me to make the sacrifice of these things, that *I am stronger now, in my eightieth year, than I was fifty years ago,* when in the habit of taking animal food, wine, strong malt liquor, spirits and water; and my bilious, my rheumatic, and my gouty complaints, I think I may say, are no more. Nor have I, since this change, ever had an attack of that most dreadful of all maladies, hypochondria. I find from continued experience (it being thirty years since I have eaten fish, flesh, or fowl, or taken fermented liquor of any kind whatever)—I find abstinence to be the best medicine ; I do not meddle with fermented liquors of any kind, even as medicine."

He then adduced his own experience when wintering in Norway and Russia, amidst ice and snow for months together, in proof of the utter fallacy of the impression that spirits are essential to preserve warmth and health of body in such regions. (The experience of Sir John Franklin, Sir John Ross, and other arctic travellers, confirms Mr. Shillitoe's opinion. So has the practice in other climates, of Charles Waterton, General Havelock, Dr. Livingstone, Rev. Robert Moffatt, and a host of others. The late indefatigable Mr. Cobden, M.P., declared " The more work I have to do, the more have I resorted to the teapot and the pump.")

Mr. Shillitoe concluded his address at Exeter Hall, by expressing his special esteem for total abstinence on religious grounds. It had lessened his own irritability, it helped men to subdue evil passions, whereas stimulants excite these and lusts which "war against the soul and render us displeasing to Almighty God."

We may suitably append to these remarks a few extracts in the same direction from an able and suggestive address, by Dr. W. E. Channing, delivered at Boston in 1837, at a meeting of American friends of temperance.

" The present occasion may well animate a Christian minister. Why is this multitude brought together, and whence comes this sympathy with the fallen, the guilty, the miserable? Have we derived it from the schools of ancient philosophy, or from the temples of Greece and Rome? No. We inherit it from Jesus Christ, we have caught it from his lips—His life—His cross. This meeting, were we to trace its origin, would carry us back to Bethlehem and Calvary.

"I begin with asking, what is the great essential evil of intemperance? The reply is given, when I say, that intemperance is the *voluntary extinction of reason.* The great evil is inward or spiritual. The intemperate man divests himself for a time of his rational or moral nature. All the other evils of intemperance are light compared with this, and almost all flow from this.

"*The* danger of this vice lies in *its almost imperceptible approach.* Few who perish by it, know its first accesses. Intemperance comes with noiseless step and binds its first cords with a touch too light to be felt. This truth of mournful experience should be treasured up by us all, and should influence the habits and arrangements of domestic and social life in every class of the community."

And in his address on self-culture, the same great man exhorts. "Above all let me urge on those who would bring out and elevate their higher nature, to abstain from the use of spirituous liquors. This bad habit is distinguished from the use of all others by the ravages it makes on the intellect. And this effect is produced to a mournful extent, *even when drunkenness is escaped.* Not a few men called temperate, and who have thought themselves such, have learned, on abstaining from the use of ardent spirits, that for years their minds had been *clouded,* impaired by moderate drinking, without their *suspecting* the injury. Multitudes in this city are bereft of half their intellectual energy by a degree of indulgence which *passes for innocent.* Of all the foes of the working class this is the deadliest. Nothing has done more to keep down this class."

# CHAPTER VIII.

GENERAL PHILANTHROPIC EFFORTS RESPECTING PRISONS, THE
SABBATH, THEATRES, AND KINDNESS TO ANIMALS.

MR. SHILLITOE did not feel himself called upon to enter
much into the question of prison management in his
own country, inasmuch as that department of philanthropic effort had been so vigorously occupied by others
who caught the fallen mantle of the illustrious Howard;
and, in particular, Mr. Thomas Fowell Buxton, Mr.
Crawford, William Allen, Dr. Lushington, Peter Bedford,
Joseph John and Samuel Gurney, and Elizabeth Fry.
But during his foreign journeys prisoners often claimed
his sympathizing attention and visitation. We can only
notice briefly a few of his principal visits of this kind.

In 1821, at Rotterdam, he, in a series of interviews
with successive groups, preached the Gospel to the inmates
of the large prison of that city, about seven hundred and fifty
in number. These being then governed by a female, styled
"the Regent," and then eighty-two years of age, were
under good discipline. The system of industrial prison-
labour, recommended by Howard, was in full operation in
that prison. The men were occupied in various branches
of handicraft and received a share of their earnings. The
women also were employed in spinning and sewing. Each
prisoner was furnished with a Bible. Thus some attention

was directed to the two main elements of criminal reformation, viz. : religious instruction, and self-help by the formation of industrial habits. A third requisite, suitable classification and separation, was not sufficiently secured at Rotterdam, owing to the construction of the building.

When, at Christmas, he visited the " slaves " or convicts in the Norwegian state prison of Aggerhuus. Afterwards, with the permission of the Governor, he drew up a further address, which was printed, and a copy presented to each prisoner. Its contents were sound. In it he spoke pointedly and satisfactorily respecting the Holy Scriptures, saying, " In the first place, let me endeavour to persuade you to cherish, as much in you lies, a disposition or desire to read the Holy Scriptures, and as frequently as suitable opportunities offer; beseeching the Almighty that He would mercifully condescend to enable you to read them to profit; as they are able to make wise unto salvation, *through faith which is in Christ Jesus,* and are given by inspiration of God, and are profitable for doctrine, for reproof, for correction, for instruction in righteousness, that the man of God may be perfect, throughly furnished unto all good works." (2 Tim. iii. 15-17.) This was much better than his discourse to the Indians at Cataragus.

By special permission of the King of Prussia, Mr. Shillitoe visited the large prisons of Spandau, near Berlin. On arrival there, the governor and officers earnestly dissuaded him from going amongst the prisoners, telling him they were so desperately violent that they might probably take his life. Undaunted and trusting in the Lord, he persisted in his resolution, addressed the prisoners collectively, and with such earnest eloquence that some of them were deeply affected. He then felt it to be his duty to shake hands with each inmate separately, as a token of Christian goodwill. This also was satisfactorily accomplished.

After his return to Berlin, he ascertained that, from fear of violence, the governor had quietly withdrawn a number of the most ferocious prisoners before introducing Mr. Shillitoe, and unknown to the latter. This produced much uneasiness in his mind, accompanied with an impression that he must make an effort to see every prisoner. For this purpose he applied to the Prime Minister, Prince Witgenstein, who, through the Minister of Justice, furnished him with a second and peremptory order to see the prisoners at Spandau without reserve.

Before starting thither again, the chief magistrate of Berlin, meeting him, exclaimed, " So you are about to make another visit to Spandau. I would wish you not to go again. Are you not afraid? Don't you know some of the prisoners murdered the last governor ? "

Undaunted by this and other discouragements, he again presented himself at the prison with his order. The governor was astounded. " For a time he appeared like a man recovering from a violent electric shock, and then again stood like a petrified subject." Mr. Shillitoe sincerely sympathised with the officials, but duty impelled him to persevere. The whole company of prisoners were now re-assembled, many of them heavily chained. He then addressed them in Christian love and with much power. The poor creatures again listened most attentively, and he records, " The countenances of many of them appeared sorrowfully affected and bathed in tears." Then, again, as before, he gave each man his hand as a parting salutation. The governor and chaplain paid many attentions to their earnest visitor on leaving. And the prisoners, collectively, entreated the chaplain to convey a message of thanks to Mr. Shillitoe from them, "and that many of them could say that the words that had been delivered amongst them reached to their very hearts, and they hoped would, in a future day, produce good fruits."

Several years afterwards Mr. Shillitoe was informed by a Prussian magistrate that his visits to Spandau had produced real and lasting results for good in the conduct of many of the prisoners, both male and female. He records, "This account felt like marrow to my bones, and awakened secret cries to the Lord my God that the praise and the glory might all be given to Him, and to Him alone."

At one of the Russian prisons Mr. Shillitoe was much affected at the sight of a party of convicts, attended by a file of soldiers, preparing to walk to Siberia, a journey which would occupy nearly a year, at the rate of fifteen miles a-day, being about four thousand miles. They were equipped with warm and thick clothing, but some of them also were compelled to walk ironed. By the clemency of the Emperor Alexander the weight of irons had been reduced from forty pounds to fourteen. Mr. Shillitoe's sympathy was deeply excited by one of the party, a young officer, who, for striking a superior, had been sentenced to banishment for life, and was to walk the whole distance to Siberia heavily ironed. His anguish was extreme. His eyelids were red with frequent weeping, and he frantically exclaimed, in Russian, from time to time, "Can nothing be done for me?" His grief arose mainly from having to part for ever from his beloved aged mother. He and the other convicts were each presented, by Mr. Shillitoe's companion, with a Testament. The young officer, on receiving his, seemed unable sufficiently to express his gratitude. On his knees he kissed the feet of the donor. After delivering a sympathising address to the party, Mr. Shillitoe adds, on leaving, " We passed the aged mother of the officer in the passage : the sight of her occasioned me an aching heart."

At the state-prison of Sing Sing, near New York, he found more than five hundred men, under apparently perfect discipline, surrounded by no walls, working in the quarries by day, and shut up in separate cells at night. Whilst together not the slightest intercommunication was permitted. At times a pin might almost be heard to drop in that large company. Mr. Shillitoe addressed these collectively, and was delighted at the good order he witnessed. From Captain Lynds, the governor, he received a most glowing account of the system pursued; and adds, very approvingly, but somewhat innocently, " On leaving this interesting establishment I could acknowledge that the one half of the order and management of it had not before been told me."

But, on turning to page 156 in the memoirs of the Rev. John Clay, the chaplain of Preston Gaol, we find an account of Captain Lynds' system, which induces one to make a discount from the impressions left on Mr. Shillitoe and his readers. Of him the author of that work writes, " This man was a notable felon-tamer. To break down and crush the prisoner's mind and will was the avowed principle on which he worked." Mr. Shillitoe certainly noticed " a few

sentinels under arms ;" but also states that "the only
punishment in use for offences is a small whip of about six
cords ;" and adds, " it is not remembered that the skin of
any of the prisoners who have undergone this punishment
has been broken by it." He further writes "of this
truly admirable institution," that "there appeared such an
air of *confidential authority* throughout the establishment,
and unaccompanied by anything like terror or dread when
the governor came in sight." Good charitable man ! Let
us, however, hear a word more from Mr. Clay, who says,
" The compulsory dumbness was all enforced by one single
instrument, the cow-hide.    Without authority, either
from governor or magistrate, the lowest felon-driver on
the establishment might condemn a prisoner to a flogging,
and execute his own sentence on the spot.    No check at all
was there placed on the under felon-tamers.    They were to
flog offenders, or beat them with thick cudgels, at their
discretion.    Again and again it was found that men (and
at one time women too) *died* from their floggings."  Some
horrible instances are then adduced by Mr. Clay, quite
sufficient to indicate that good Mr. Shillitoe was, at least,
somewhat imposed upon at Sing Sing.  And, notwithstanding the free access granted him for a religious address
to the prisoners, it appears from Mr. Clay that " Captain
Lynds openly proclaimed his disbelief in the possibility of
religious reformation."   This, alone, is amply sufficient
to account for the ultimate collapse of his system.   It is
but fair to add, that of later years Sing Sing prison has
been under excellent management.

Another American prison visited by Mr. Shillitoe was
the Philadelphia State Prison for Pennsylvania.  That is a

truly admirable institution. There the three real essentials of good prison management are, more or less, united; essentials which separately are failures, but which, in proper combination, afford the maximum of attainable success ; viz., industrial training, due separation, and religious instruction.

Some of Mr. Shillitoe's life-long labours in promotion of Sabbath observance have been already alluded to. But it will be appropriate to notice them also a little further, inasmuch as they formed a characteristic feature in his career.

In 1808 he published, and widely circulated, a general address to the influential classes in the nation, in which he called particular attention to the unnecessary travelling on the Sabbath, and to the evils of Sunday newspapers. Of these, he added, " They are *not* ' little things ' if they obstruct our being found in the discharge of our duty to our Maker, and will, no doubt, if pursued, ultimately tend to greater evils."

In 1817, at Sheffield, he personally visited the individual subscribers to the news-rooms there, for the purpose of inducing them to close it on the Sabbath. At other places he made similar efforts on various occasions.

At Hamburg and Altona, as already mentioned, his efforts for Sabbath observance were very vigorous, and led to his imprisonment for a night. In seeking to call the attention of an influential person at Hamburg to the condition of its public morals, he received a response embodying a principle which, in his zealous endeavours, he sometimes appears to have overlooked, viz., " The devil must first be cast out, and then, if the *heart* is pure, the *fruit* will be good." Throughout life Mr. Shillitoe attached an exaggerated value to external regulations. Doubtless, he effected some good in this direction, but if he had proclaimed the root principles of the fear of an omniscient God and the love of a gracious Saviour, more often and prominently as the chief essential, then greater success might have resulted in the way of permanent and hearty obedience.

In Norway, Denmark, and Germany, he was much grieved at the lax ideas of the Lutheran clergy respecting the Sabbath. Many of these justified, both by precept and example, the frequenting of balls and concerts on the Sabbath afternoons and evenings. In many interviews with bishops and clergymen, he earnestly protested against the mischievous influence of such sanction to evil, and urged upon them their fearful responsibilities to God at the great day of final account.

In one of these interviews (with the Bishop of Christiania) he met with a very pleasant reception. That dignitary, on being urged to use his influence with the King in favour of a better observance of the Sabbath, replied, "I can, and I will do it." Mr. Shillitoe then, in a friendly but respectful manner, laying his hands on the Bishop's shoulders, said, " I now feel the load which I have so long travelled under, taken off my shoulders, and placed where it properly belongs, on thine." Then, after further more agreeable intercourse, the Bishop took leave of him with the words, " I greet you most friendly, and wish you a good journey, and that the peace and blessing of God may follow you everywhere."

In various parts of France and Switzerland he made

strenuous efforts to induce the governors and magistrates to suppress Sabbath abuses.

The mayor of Congenies, in the South of France, at Mr. Shillitoe's petition, authoritatively closed the dancing-rooms there on Sundays, whereupon the young men of the town united in expostulations at being deprived of their usual enjoyment. They not succeeding in moving the mayor, the young women went to him in a body, and their leader, on her knees, begged for a relaxation of the prohibition. The worthy official politely but firmly adhered to his decision, and when Mr. Shillitoe again called to thank him for his faithfulness, expressed his determination to abide by his policy throughout the term of his mayoralty.

The Protestant pastor at Congenies being in the habit of uniting with his young people at playing bowls, after the Sabbath service, Mr. Shillitoe visited him to express his deep regret at such an example. It was urged in reply that, for about four hundred years, this custom had been regularly practised, and the apostolic precept, " Rejoice with them that do rejoice," was also quoted in defence. But his visitor decidedly protested against such an interpretation of that text, and left the pastor evidently somewhat uneasy with his Sabbath example.

Mr. Shillitoe, in a series of personal interviews, laid before the Archbishop of Canterbury, the Bishop of London, and the stipendiary magistrates at the metropolitan police courts, his deep regret at the abuse of the Sabbath in and around London, and besought them to make active exertions for effecting a better state of things. In these visits he was, in general, received with much courtesy, but it does not appear that very definite results ensued.

And in most of his interviews with sovereigns and influential persons, the suppression of Sabbath abuses formed a prominent portion of his representations and requests.

In like manner theatres and dramatic performances received from him all the opposition he could bring to bear upon them ; and, in some instances, he was successful in effecting their suspension.    Thus, during his stay at Barnsley, in 1816, he entered upon a vigorous campaign against the proprietors of the theatre there.    They publicly ridiculed the good Quaker on the stage, and personated his dress and appearance.    But he persevered in his opposition, wrote tracts against the evils of plays, and widely distributed them.    He was, eventually, able to record, with thankfulness to God, their utter discomfiture, and the cessation of the theatre, whose effects on public morals had so grieved him.    " Their prospects were so defeated they were obliged to leave the town, it was said much worse than they came to it; they made several attempts after this to obtain supporters, but in vain.    The theatre was afterwards converted into a dissenting meeting-house."    Such was the triumph of conscientious individual influence !

In an interview at Copenhagen with the Princess Royal of Denmark, after hearing Mr. Shillitoe's regrets at the patronage accorded to theatres and other gaieties by the clergy, she admitted the fact, and replied, " We do not see that improvement in the morals of the people which is so desirable ; for some of the clergy now take liberties which were not formerly practised, by attending the theatre and other places of amusement, whereby their

example unfits them for the usefulness which they otherwise might exert amongst the people. And that is not
all. Is it to be expected, if they are sent for to attend
upon the sick, that they can be in a fit state of mind to go
from the theatre or ball-room to visit the bedside of such?
I think not."

Even dumb animals often participated in his beneficent
exertions. In his memoranda he repeatedly records his
kindly interest in their comfort and humane treatment.
And where cases of cruelty came under his observation,
he would take considerable pains to draw official attention
to them. Thus, when at Nismes, he was much pained to
learn that the sport of bull-baiting was constantly indulged
in there. Having, therefore, obtained an introduction to
the Catholic Bishop, he entreated his interference in the
matter. That prelate, however, declined to exert himself,
saying, "I have nothing to do with you. You are not
in my jurisdiction, and I do not want any of your instruction." He then abruptly dismissed him, with much
displeasure manifest on his countenance. On arriving in
Paris, Mr. Shillitoe sought an interview with the Archbishop respecting the bull-baiting; but that functionary
would not grant him an interview.

On another occasion, when in Ireland, he learnt that
the same barbarous sport was practised at Waterford. As
he understood that the Protestant Bishop of that city had
much influence with the authorities, he waited upon him,
and urged his interposition. This, the Bishop cheerfully
promised, and treated his visitor with much consideration
and respect. When Mr. Shillitoe afterwards returned to
Waterford, he was gratified to find that in the interval the
bull-baiting had been discontinued.

L

# CHAPTER IX.

## LAST DAYS.

EVENING OF LIFE AT TOTTENHAM—EFFORTS FOR HIS POOR
NEIGHBOURS — HIS EXTENSIVE CORRESPONDENCE — LETTER
FROM PROFESSOR THOLUCK — REVIVAL AMONGST THE
FRIENDS—INDISPENSABLE NECESSITY FOR CHRIST'S SPIRI-
TUAL INFLUENCES ON THE SOUL, AS OBTAINED BY A CONSTANT
LOOKING TO THE CROSS—CHRIST FAITHFUL AND TRUE FROM
YOUTH TO AGE—QUOTATION FROM DR. BONAR—PREPARED
AND EXTEMPORANEOUS COMMUNICATIONS—HABITUAL REVE-
RENCE—LAST EXPRESSIONS AND FINALLY SUSTAINING HOPES
OF THOMAS SHILLITOE.

AFTER his return, in 1829, from the long American
journey, at the age of nearly seventy-six, Thomas Shillitoe
quietly settled down at Tottenham again, where during the
few remaining years of his life he still occupied himself
with such benevolent and religious services as his failing
strength permitted him to undertake.

The poorer inhabitants of Tottenham and its neighbourhood now obtained a considerable portion of his sympathizing efforts, and he devoted much time to personal
visitation amongst them. His homely manners and humble
simplicity rendered him a great favourite amongst them;
and they gladly welcomed the brisk footstep and cheery
voice of the active little man, as he came towards them
with his habitual liveliness and freedom.

The better accommodation of the aged poor claimed

much of his attention in these, his declining years, and, old as he was, he undertook to raise a fund for an extensive addition to the almshouse accommodation of the place. He often visited his rich neighbours to solicit contributions for these and kindred works of charity, and, emboldened by the intrinsic worth of the objects, he was very persevering in his requisitions. It was not his custom to entreat, so much as to demand, in a good-humoured way, the needful aid for his poor clients. "I want such and such a sum of money," was his frequent salutation to his wealthy and philanthropic acquaintances. And, as it was well-known that "Thomas will not take 'No' for an answer," he generally obtained his requests pretty readily.

The high estimation in which he was held by all who knew him, made his way easy in such matters. Not merely the Friends, but persons of all denominations, loved and honoured him. It was the remark of a neighbouring clergyman of the Church of England, on hearing of his decease, "A better man never lived."

On one occasion, when calling at the residence of a wealthy gentleman at Tottenham, he found, on enquiry, that the owner was not at home; but his lady, hearing who it was that wanted him, invited Thomas in, and said, "Now, Mr. Shillitoe, I shall be happy to assist you; for my husband left instructions that, whenever you called on your benevolent errands, I was to supply you with whatever you might ask for." Thomas named the sum he desired, and at once received it accordingly. And thus it happened in many similar instances.

Some of these kindly solicitations were made on behalf

of pious persons whom, in the course of his travels, he had ascertained to be in needy circumstances. Thus, in looking over his papers recently, the writer came across a very grateful acknowledgment of pecuniary help collected by him, on his return to England, for an aged and necessitous minister of the gospel, whom he had met in America. Such services appear to have been often rendered by him to persons both at home and abroad. There is now lying before the writer a letter from a young Englishman at Lisbon, addressed to Mr. Shillitoe, and warmly expressing his appreciation of his character and kindness.

Another similar letter from a person at Berlin recurs with grateful satisfaction to his Prussian visit, and his services there to individuals, as well as to public gatherings. The writer says—

" Last summer I was in Pyrmont with our social friend, Louis Seebohm. I felt very comfortable in the society of his dear family. Mrs. Seebohm, a very sincere and amiable woman, led me, soon after my arrival, into her own room, to show me your picture. They spoke with great love of you; and in our conversation we often joined in praising the gracious providence of God, who brought you, an old man, from a far and foreign country, here to proclaim the Lord full of goodness and mercy to poor deeply-fallen creatures, who, in former times, were not taught thus to love and adore Him.

" I am sure your visit to Berlin, and especially, the attention you paid to the prisoners, has been of very great benefit; for since that time there has been formed a society for instructing and amending the prisoners.

There are some very pious young preachers appointed to visit the prisoners regularly every day, and the members of the society endeavour to bring those who are dismissed from the prison to some useful employment, and keep a watchful eye upon their conduct."

It was the writer of the above letter who, when he met religious persons from London, used to enquire, after the manner of Joseph in Egypt, "Doth my father Shillitoe still live?"

Mr. Shillitoe's home and foreign correspondence was an extensive one. Whilst abroad on his journeys he was desirous of being kept fully informed of the movements and welfare of his intimate friends at home. Accordingly, two of his acquaintances, Joseph Allen and Josiah Forster, were in the habit of regularly forwarding to him closely-written folios filled with minutely detailed narrations of home news. These, on their receipt in distant parts, were read with great interest by the good man to whom they were addressed.

As an illustration of the high esteem conceived for this simple, uneducated, but thoroughly devoted Christian, by many of the great and learned ones amongst whom he came, we may appropriately quote a few extracts from a hitherto unpublished letter addressed to him by one of the most eminent theologians and scholars of Germany—Professor Tholuck.

"The hours which I passed in your company have left upon my mind an indelible impression; I tasted fully the sweetness of the presence of Christ, who will always manifest Himself where His disciples meet in sincerity and with a longing after His grace. Your letters have contribute to impress the remembrance of those hours still deeper in my mind, and, as long as I live, I shall remember you as an experienced disciple of Christ, whom I shall one day meet with before the Throne of Grace.

"As to my opinion of Quakerism, I consider the Friends as real, sound Christians, who are right in several points, but erroneous in a greater number of things, owing chiefly to a false interpretation of Scripture. The little tract, ' On silent waiting upon God,' has met with my full approval; yet I cannot persuade myself that this is the only way of worshipping Him rightly. On the contrary, loud thanksgiving and imploring is, according to my opinion, not less agreeable to my Saviour than a quiet looking up to Him. I cannot deny that thousands of Church-people attribute too much value to the external forms of worship, without keeping their heart open to the eternal stream that flows, conditionally, down into the hearts of all those that listen to Divine things.

"A chief point with you is the article of the Lord's Supper. As to this, I readily believe that you may feel at times in as lively a manner the communion with Christ, as any body of those who take the sacrament; but to avoid taking it is against Scripture, whatever may be said against it by the masters of your sect. Christ wanted to give us an external form, with which He connected the promise of sending the Spirit too, as soon as it was properly used. I cannot see, therefore, why we should not use an external ceremony which Christ may bless so graciously as to become the means of spiritual awakening aud edification. It appears to me to be ungrateful not to use those instruments of grace which the Lord recommended to us.

Certainly He would not have recommended them, had He known we are stronger than we really are. But as He knew that we want such external helps, we cannot contradict His knowledge of our weakness.

"However, with me all the disputed points between the Church-people and the Friends are no material points of Christianity. The one great material point of Christianity is the vital belief that we are saved by the *free mercy* of God, through the life and the death of our blessed Redeemer. Where this belief is an experimental one, where sin has been felt in its full extent and horribleness, and, afterwards, Christ, in His sweetness to the poor helpless sinner, the good fruit of this belief will shoot forth necessarily. And with whomsoever this vital belief is found, he is a child of God, and accepted in the Beloved One, may his peculiar opinions be whatever they will. That foundation is then laid which no fire will consume, although the by-work may all be burnt up with eternal fire.

"I trust, my dear paternal friend, we both are built on that foundation. Let us, therefore, remain united in Him who first led us to each other, in our beloved Redeemer, Jesus Christ."

Such free and loving communication was very interesting to Mr. Shillitoe, and many such friendly letters were received by him, both from Professor Tholuck and other Christians of various denominations at home and aboad.

Meanwhile, the good old man, after his long and arduous pilgrimage, found a most welcome repose in the circle of his affectionate family, who had, through the Lord's blessing, settled comfortably in life, and acquired for themselves useful and honourable positions in society.

Mr. Shillitoe's wife, his faithful partner in so long and happy a union, survived her husband about two years, when, with prayer and thanksgiving, she passed away to her Saviour at the ripe age of ninety-two.

To the very last, Mr. Shillitoe was a diligent and punctual attender at public worship. He was especially interested in attending funerals, inasmuch as the solemn impressions often felt on such occasions were very favourable for the profitable reception of his ministerial discourses. And on these occasions his preaching was often felt to be deep and thorough,—going to the root of evil in the heart. And this is ever needful. For, even in the religious world, there is often little appreciation of the wide distinction between *holiness* and common *virtue*, and of the *merely* artificial separation between *sin* and *crime*.

Holiness is an affectionate and really *hearty* submission to Christ's commands, as well as practical trust in His love and sacrificial death. According to the uncompromising terms of the Bible, sin is whatever is *secretly* opposed to God's will and spirit. Much that is abomination in His sight is counted virtuous and creditable in so-called respectable society, and in many religious circles, and even amongst the authorities of the churches at times. Crime is the transgression of mere human law, and, in general, society reserves its indignation for this, whilst it regards with complacency many things which possess far greater intrinsic evil in the Divine sight. But the Great Day will reverse many of these respectable human decisions, and display in the unescapable sunlight of Christ all sin and all sinners as regarded in *His* estimate, and *not*, as heretofore, regarded by human consideration.

Mr. Shillitoe's declining years witnessed the commencement of a lively religious revival amongst his dear brethren,
the Friends. The occurrence of the Hicksite heresy in
America, was a means of rousing up the Society in
Great Britain to a greatly increased care, to pay due
honour to the blessed Scriptures given forth by the Holy
Spirit, and to bear a yet clearer testimony to the efficacy and
necessity of faith in the atoning sacrifice and death of the
Lord Jesus Christ. This revival has manifested, in a
striking manner, the influence which the clear setting
forth of the Gospel of Christ has upon social as well
as upon individual energies. For since the incarnation
and self-sacrificing love of the Redeemer have thus been
set forth with such increased frequency amongst the
Friends, their community has been constrained to a remarkable growth in every good work, but especially in
home and foreign missions, and in the instruction of poor
and neglected children. The Lord Jesus Christ has been
thus experienced to be life as well as light.

Yet not the less has the blessed scriptural doctrine of
the Holy Spirit been precious to them. This was,
throughout his life, a favourite topic with Thomas
Shillitoe. And, as his days drew to a close, he again
and again urged upon his friends the necessity for the
positive reception of this real and ever-renewed communication from the Lord to the heart of every believer in
Christ, as his daily spiritual food, his indispensable support for the duties and difficulties of life. This gracious
gift is to be implored by fervent prayer, and in connection with a diligent use of His most habitual and most
honoured channel of communication, the reverent and

meditative contemplation of Christ's person and work by the habitual perusal of His own words in the Holy Scriptures.

For there is a constant and inseparable connection between the love of Christ, as the once suffering but now risen Saviour, and the reception of the higher manifestations of His Holy Spirit. The Christian progress is not merely begun by the Lord Jesus, and then carried forward by the Holy Spirit apart from Him. There must be an ever-renewed recurrence to the great love of Him, who said, " I lay down my life for the sheep. *No man taketh it from Me,* but I lay it down of Myself." (John x.) It is mainly and permanently the love and worship of Jesus which *brings* the Holy Spirit down. To obtain and deepen that love there must be frequent recurrence to the Gospel narrations of it. For "faith cometh by *hearing*, and hearing by the word of God."

Our limited space precludes the quotation of any of Thomas Shillitoe's addresses on this subject; but in the excellent "Treatise on Prayer," by Edward Bicker-steth, there is given so condensed and complete a view of this important doctrine, that it may be very suitably introduced here :—

" Especially the Holy Spirit sheds abroad the love of God in our hearts, taking of the things of Christ and showing them to us, and so effectually drawing our hearts out in full confidence and love to the throne of grace. The gift and intercession of the Holy Spirit is the fruit and effect of the intercession of Christ, who, when He ascended up on high, led captivity captive, and received this gift for men ; yea, even for the rebellious.

"Much, indeed, of the work of the Spirit is secret. We know not various particulars connected with it. We know it rather by *its effects* than by its mode of operation. 'The wind bloweth where it listeth, and thou hearest the sound thereof, but canst not tell whence it cometh, and whither it goeth: so is every one that is born of the Spirit.' We experience His power, and that is sufficient. The Christian knows that he has often knelt down averse to prayer—dead, dull, stupid; almost without desiring the blessings for which he ought to ask. And yet with all his weakness, after looking for the aid of the Spirit, after praying, as did David, 'Lord, open Thou my lips, and my mouth shall show forth Thy praise' (Psalm li. 15), and persevering in asking, seeking, and knocking (Matt. vii. 7), he has in such a remarkable way experienced the presence of God, as to fill him with joy unspeakable, and a hope full of glory. He has in these cases sometimes found an unction, an enlargement of expression, so far beyond anything that he had previously calculated upon, or could expect, accompanied by such lively and vehement desires and thirstings after God, and holiness, and glory, as satisfactorily and evidently, to his mind, marked the agency and assistance of a Divine power, which maketh intercession for us."

In his frequent sermons on the indispensable necessity for the abiding operations of the Holy Spirit, Thomas Shillitoe at times alluded to the blessedness and privilege of thus experiencing God to be a faithful and permanently unchanging Father to His humble children, tenderly guarding them from youth to age, and often enabling them, in the later stages of life, to recur with reverent

thankfulness to a long and unbroken succession of
solemnizing visitation from the days of childhood onwards.
It is indeed a precious thing in advancing years to be able
thus to realize the Lord Jesus Christ as " the same
yesterday, to-day, and for ever ;" as the dearest and most
faithful One, unchangeable and immortal, not only the
God of childhood and youth, but as affording also an ever-
sustaining and renewing energy amid the cares and vicis-
situdes of middle life; and at a still later period again
enabling His children to realize a cheering personal meaning in the prophecy—" At evening-time it shall be light."
(Zech. xiv. 7).

In connection with Thomas Shillitoe's frequent sermons
and letters on the Holy Spirit's operations, some notice
appears needful of an opinion which he held, in common
with some other good men of his sect, tending to limit
the blessings of the Holy Spirit, in public preaching,
exclusively to extempore discourses.  Thus he sometimes
spoke of manuscript and premeditated sermons as being
merely "hashed up," and assumed as of universal and
permanent application the words specially addressed to
the Apostles, and under special circumstances—"Take no
thought how or what ye shall speak, for it shall be given
you in that same hour what ye shall speak."  Herein he
unintentionally ignored some of God's best gifts to men,
as scriptural research, memory, reason, and prayerful
preparation for work.  And herein, too, he was singularly
inconsistent with himself; for he often drew up religious
addresses, which were neither more nor less than manuscript prepared sermons, the very things which, under
another name, and when read from a pulpit, he deprecated

as "hashed up." George Fox, too, was a constant pre-
parer of written sermons, but which he called his religious
"epistles." There may be, and ought to be, quite as
much prayerful dependence on the aid and blessing of
God in writing a book or a religious document as in any
oral address. Indeed, the former requires *far more* care
and dependence, being more permanent in form than the
latter, and often very much wider in extent of diffusion
and influence. Anthony Norris Groves, a founder of the
Plymouth Brethren, deprecated this objection to all prepared discourses, as being virtually a "commanding to
abstain from meats which God hath created to be received
with thanksgiving." For the faculties of prayerful
religious composition, apt quotation and appropriate
illustration, are indeed "meats" given for use, and not for
disuse. Their right application implies entire dependence
upon God. We are also entirely dependent upon Him for
our outward "meat" or food. Yet we labour for it,
produce it, grow it, and then prepare it. And in *all* these
processes we are dependent wholly upon God, and not
merely in its final reception.

Doubtless, extempore discourses are best on many
occasions, but there are also many other occasions when
properly prepared addresses are superior and more appropriate. Each kind has its right place, time, and function,
and neither should be exalted at the expense of the other.
Dr. Horatius Bonar, in his excellent little work, " God's
Way of Holiness," (London : Nisbet & Co.) appropriately
says, " The Holy Spirit does not destroy or reverse man's
faculties ; He renovates them *all*, so that they fulfil the
true ends for which they were given. As He does not

make the hand the foot, nor the eye the ear, so He does not make the heart the intellect, nor the will the judgment. Each faculty remains the same in end and use as before, only purified and set properly to work. Nor does the Holy Spirit supersede the use of our faculties by His indwelling. Rather does this indwelling make these more serviceable, more energetic, each one doing his *proper* work, and fulfilling his proper office."

In the same work of Dr. Bonar's is a brief and excellent statement, relative to the permanent connection between the Christian's indispensable recurrence to the Scripture records of the dying love of our Lord Jesus, and the reception of the influences of His Holy Spirit. From its connection with the correct, and also with the defective, views of Thomas Shillitoe on the subject, we may quote it here :—

"He who would know holiness, must understand *sin ;* and He who would see sin, *as God sees it*, and think of it as God does, must look at the cross and grave of the Son of God, must know the meaning of Gethsemane and Golgotha.

" Of spiritual health *the Cross* is the source. From it there goes forth the virtue, the power, that heals all maladies, be they slight or deadly. For, ' *by his stripes* we are healed,' and in Him we find ' the tree of life' with its healing leaves. Golgotha has become Gilead, with its skilful physician and its bruised balm. The cure is not perfected in an hour. But as the sight of the Cross begins it, *so does it complete it*, at last. Yes, the Cross heals. It possesses the double virtue of killing sin and quickening holiness. Thus, looking to the Cross, each day as at the first, we are made sensible of the restoration of our soul's health; evil loosens its hold, while good strengthens and ripens. The Cross is strength for activity or for endurance, for holiness as well as for work. He that would be holy or useful, must *keep* near the Cross.

" He that would be like Christ, moreover, must *study* Him. We cannot make ourselves holy by merely *trying* to be so, any more than we can make ourselves believe and love by simple energy of endeavour. No force can effect this. Men *try* to be holy, and they fail. They cannot by direct effort work themselves into holiness. They must gaze upon a holy object; and so be changed into its likeness 'from glory to glory.' They must have a holy Being for their bosom friend. Companionship with Jesus, like that of John, can alone make us resemble either the disciple or the Master. He that would be holy must steep himself in the word, must bask in the sunshine which radiates from each page of revelation."

But Satan exerts special influence to draw away Christians from thus looking to Him, "by whose *stripes we* are healed." Earnest frequent prayer is essential for deliverance from the invisible but mischievous power of the hateful being who still persecutes the righteous with outward trials and inward assaults, as he did Job of old, and who still seems to sift God's people as wheat, " desiring to have " them, as in Peter's case. Christ prayed for Peter that the Devil might not succeed with him. So also we must pray for similar Divine protection from him.

As Thomas Shillitoe drew nearer and nearer to the sunset of life, his views of the pre-eminent power of the Cross appear to have become clearer and deeper. Nowhere

in his recorded expressions are the references to Christ's
dying love, to His free, unmerited, unpurchaseable, un-
deserved, and undeservable grace, so frequent as in the
last days of his pilgrimage.   And thus it has been with
all good men, in proportion as they have grown in real
wisdom and Christian experience.

And we must here say a word of one characteristic of
him, which has not been mentioned in the preceding
pages,—his habitual *reverence* and holy fear of God.   In
heart and habitual feeling, and always in his preaching,
he was thus reverent, ever conscious that the Omniscient
Lord is a Great King, " the High and Holy One that
inhabiteth eternity," " who humbleth Himself to behold
the things which are in heaven and in earth."   Yet, how
often is this holy reverence lacking even in well-intentioned
men, and in not a few who claim to be ministers and
servants of God?   " The fear of the Lord is the beginning
of wisdom ; " and not the beginning only, but it deepens
and increases, as true wisdom deepens in the soul.   The
ripe corn bows its head as it ripens.   In speaking and
thinking of our Lord Jesus Christ, we should ever
remember that He is the Son and image of that infinite
Almighty Deity whose created dominions embrace worlds
upon worlds, and universe upon universe—infinities so
sublime that our earth and all its inhabitants would no
more be missed therefrom, if annihilated, than one single
leaf taken from the foliage of a mighty forest.   Paul fell
to the ground before Christ at Damascus.   The wrapt
Isaiah trembled at a glimpse of His glory.   And even the
once familiarly affectionate John, when, after the Ascension, he was again visited in vision by his beloved Lord,

" fell at His feet as dead." Seeing, then, how faithful Prophets and Apostles thus felt their nothingness before the mighty Godhead of the Lord Jesus and of His Father, how much more is an abiding reverence needful and seemly for each one of us!

Thomas Shillitoe was able to continue his ministry and charitable visits, until two or three weeks before his decease; and, throughout his last brief illness, he was permitted to enjoy the blessing of an unclouded mind, a privilege not always accorded in dying hours. When he finally entered " the valley of the shadow of death " (only the *shadow*), the glories of the Heavenly City shone, by believing anticipation, brightly and continuously over his faithful spirit.

Amongst his last utterances were the following, " I am in the hands of a merciful God. Take me; I can give up all in this world. Oh, come, come blessed Jesus! if it is consistent with Thy blessed will. Into Thy careful keeping, into Thy merciful hands, I commit my dear children, and my dear grandchildren, All-merciful! " " Oh send, if consistent with Thy holy will, send my release. O heavenly Father, be pleased, if consistent with Thy blessed will, to say, ' This is enough.' Send, send, O merciful Father, help, that I may not let go my confidence."

Then addressing himself to his friends, he exclaimed, " Oh, assist me with your prayers, that I may be released from the shackles of mortality. My love is to everybody, the wicked and all; I love *them*, but not their *ways*. I truly know sorrow as to the *body*, but not as to the *mind*. Oh! my *head* aches, but not my *heart*. Oh, bear with

M

me, if I am impatient; the restlessness of the body, but not of the mind, you can have no conception of."

To his dear aged partner he spoke most affectionately, even in the very agonies of dissolution, and expressed a wish that they might both be buried in the same grave.

Speaking of his bright hope of the realization of the glorious days hereafter, so frequently depicted in the glowing anticipations of Prophets and Apostles, he said, whilst in his last illness, " Oh, let it be known that I contend to the last with unremitting confidence and assurance for the second coming of our Lord and Saviour Jesus Christ to the saving of the soul."

And here we may observe that an animating hope of the future blessings of Christ's millennial and post-millennial Kingdom, which was so characteristic a feature of the early Christians,* and which sustained them joyfully amid even torture and martyrdom, needs to be more prominently and frequently urged upon modern Christians, than has hitherto been done in these latter ages. Happily, it is now receiving more attention, and is being inculcated by the most religious persons of various denominations. How often did the Apostles allude to this second coming of the Lord, when, in infinite majesty, He should descend with His saints to raise His faithful ones, to establish His personal Kingdom, to restore the throne of David in

---

* Justin Martyr, one of the earliest and most eminent of the Christian Fathers, writing about 100 years after our Lord's ascension, says, " I however, and as many as are altogether orthodox, believe that there will be a resurrection of the flesh and a Millennium, in Jerusalem restored, adorned, and enlarged, according to the predictions of Ezekiel, Isaiah, and the other Prophets."

perpetual splendour, ruling thereon Himself, over Jew
and Gentile, in the endless blessedness predicted of the
" times of restitution of all things," when, eventually,
" new heavens and a new earth " shall have been created,
when the holy City, the heavenly Jerusalem, shall have
finally descended from God, and when " the name of the
City, from that day, shall be, ' The Lord is there.' "
(Ezek. lxviii. 35 ; Rev. xxi. 1-3.)

With this glorious promise our Lord rose from Olivet ;
and as He ascended from the scene of the solemn triumph
of His incarnation, there sounded from the celestial voices
of attendant angels the sustaining words of a new joy and
hope for men. " This *same* Jesus, who is taken up from
you into heaven, shall *so* come *in like manner* as *ye* have
seen Him go into heaven."

And evermore the illimitable triumphs of that Kingdom
of perfect holiness, and of the purest beneficence, will be
permeated with the precious influences and memories of
the Cross. Even amid celestial splendour, even in the
centre of the throne of the Highest, was seen " *a Lamb as
it had been slain.*" Both in millennial times, and in the
blissful ages following thereafter for ever, the Great King
will be He who declared to His beloved disciple in Patmos,
" I am He that liveth and *was dead*, and behold I am
alive for evermore. Amen." For beneath the thin veil
of that sacred body that suffered on Calvary, even now
the eye of faith discerns the awful majesty of Him before
whom the grandest angels reverently bow,—the Everlasting Father, the Lord God Almighty.

As has been already alluded to, Thomas Shillitoe in his
dying hours repeatedly confessed his own sinfulness and

unworthiness.  Again and again he acknowledged that all
was of pure unmerited grace through the love and sufferings of the divine Jesus.  More than once he said, "All
that ever I have done is but as filthy rags."  Thus humbly
trusting, he could add, "Mine eyes have seen Thy salvation and Thy glory; when shall I feel Thy presence?"

Consistently with this abiding confidence, his last
recorded words were a prayer to his Redeemer and King,
"Oh, holy, blessed Jesus!  be with me in this awful
moment.  Come, oh, come, and receive me to Thyself.
And of Thine own free mercy, in Thine own time, admit
me into Thy heavenly Kingdom!"

In his sense of entire emptiness of independent
merit or goodness, he exemplified the words of Martin
Boos, "They are dearer to God that seek something *from*
Him than they that seek to bring something *to* Him."

> "Among My saints, behold Me stand
>     As one that *serveth* still;
> No ministration at their hand
>     My purpose may fulfil.
>
> *Nor can they aught to Me impart*
>     Save that I seek a broken heart;
> Each day the *debt* must *greater* be,
>     *Swelling throughout eternity.*"

Thus self-renouncing, thus wholly leaning upon Christ,
thus looking forward to the grand Kingdom of the future
age, Thomas Shillitoe closed his eyes in the slumber of
death, and was gathered to the innumerable host of saints,
of whom the Apostle speaks as being in like manner "fallen
asleep" till the morning of the Resurrection, when their
Lord will raise them to the endless glorious life.

# ILLUSTRATED BOOKS

## Presents and Distribution.

S. W. PARTRIDGE, 9, Paternoſter Row.

# ANIMAL SAGACITY.

A selection of remarkable Incidents illustrative of the Sagacity of Animals. In prose and verse. Edited by Mrs. S. C. HALL. Cloth, 5s., cloth, gilt edges, 7s. 6d.

## CONTENTS.

The Three Bears; Miss Bruin.—"Charlie," the White Sergeant.—Tommy's Clever Trick.—The Lion, the King of the Forest; Danco.—Gipsy and the Chickens.—The Elephant and Cobblers.—Old Zeb.—The Chaffinches and the Nest.—The Whip of Straw.—Faithful Chum.—Affection of Sheep. —Sagacity of Cats.—Rover's One Fault.—Sagacity of the Rat.—Robin Redbreast.—The Dog and the Nightingale.—Dogs Preserving Property and Life.—Our Noble "Friend."—The Docility and Affection of the Horse.— Fidelity of the Dog.—"Lab" and the Canary.—Dandie; or, the Dog that could reason.—The Cat and the Blackbird.—A Dog that was kind to his fellow.—Dogs Saving Life.—Meggy's Grave, &c.

---

NEW WORK BY DR. NEWTON.

# THE GREAT PILOT

AND

# HIS LESSONS.

By the Rev. RICHARD NEWTON, D.D., author of "The Giants," &c.

## CONTENTS.

Mary's Choice; or, The Good Portion.—Doing for Jesus.—The Best Ornament.—The Prince of Peace.—The Best Friend.—The Secret of Safety.— The Best Name.—A Tree of Life.—A Heavenly Home.

With many Engravings. Cloth, 1s. 6d.

---

London: S. W. PARTRIDGE, 9, Paternoster Row.

OUR

# DUMB COMPANIONS;

*Or, Conversations about*

## DOGS, HORSES, DONKEYS, AND CATS.

By THOMAS JACKSON, M.A.

With Seventy-five Engravings.    Cloth, 5s., cloth extra, 7s. 6d.

[*Third Edition.*

---

OUR

# CHILDREN'S    PETS;

In Prose and Verse.  By JOSEPHINE.  With Seventy Engravings.  Cloth, 5s.
cloth extra, 7s. 6d.

[*Second Edition*

---

# SHORT STEPS FOR LITTLE FEET.

By the Author of "The Children's Party,"  With Ten Engravings.  Cover
printed in Colours, 1s.

[" *Children's Friend* " *Series.*

---

London : S. W. PARTRIDGE, 9, Paternoster Row.

**A GOLDEN YEAR; and its Lessons of Labour.**
By the Author of " Marian Falconer." With Six Engravings. Cloth,
2s. 6d. [*Second Edition.*

---

**SPARKS FROM THE ANVIL.** By Elihu
Burritt. With many Engravings. Revised by the Author. With a new
Preface. Cloth, 1s. 6d. [*New Edition.*

---

**A KISS FOR A BLOW;** or a Collection of Stories
for Children. By H. C. Wright. With Eight Illustrations by H.
Anelay, Esq. Cloth, 1s. 6d. [*New Edition.*

---

**THE STORY OF LITTLE ALFRED.** By D. J. E.,
Author of " Story of the Lost London." With many Engravings. Cloth, 1s.
[*Second Edition.*

---

**JOHN HEPPELL;** "or, Just One Glass." With
Eight Engravings. Cloth, 1s.

---

**THE CLIFF HUT;** or, the Perils of a Fisherman's
Family. By Miss Bakewell, Author of " Hannah Twist." With many
Illustrations. Cloth, 1s.

---

**THE VOICE OF CHILDHOOD;** or, the influence
and the poetry, the wrongs and the wants of our Little Ones. By John de
Fraine. With Eight Engravings. Cloth, 6d. [*Second Edition.*

---

**HOW PAUL'S PENNY BECAME A POUND.**
By the Author of " Dick and his Donkey." With Twelve Engravings.
Cover printed in *colours*, 1s. [" *Children's Friend* " *Series.*

---

**HOW PETER'S POUND BECAME A PENNY.**
By the Author of " Dick and his Donkey." With Twelve Engravings.
Cover printed in *colours*, 1s.
[" *Children's Friend* " *Series.*

---

London : S. W. PARTRIDGE, 9, Paternoster Row.

# ILLUSTRATED PENNY READINGS.

*Nos. 1 to 12, done up in cloth, 1/6; paper boards, 1/; packets, 1/.*

## "British Workman" Placards.

### One Penny; Coloured, Threepence.

*Nos. 1 to 12, done up in packet, One Shillimg.*

\*\*\* If an order be sent with fourteen stamps, the complete set will be forwarded post free.

London: S. W. PARTRIDGE, 9, Paternoster Row.

**RONALD'S REASON;** *or, the Little*
Cripple. A Book for Boys. By Mrs. S. C. HALL. With TEN Engravings, 1s. One of "*The Children's Friend*" Series.

---

**SYBIL & HER LIVE SNOWBALL.**
By the Author of "Dick and his Donkey." A Book for Girls. With TWELVE Engravings, 1s. One of "*The Children's Friend*" Series.

---

**TALK WITH THE LITTLE ONES.**
A Book for Boys and Girls. By the Author of "Rhymes Worth Remembering." With THIRTY Engravings, 1s. One of "*The Children's Friend*" Series.

---

**ROGER MILLER;** *or, Heroism in Humble*
Life. By the Rev. GEO. ORME. With an Engraving, cloth, 1s. 6d.
[*New Edition.*

---

**PETER BEDFORD,** *the Spitalfields Philan-*
thropist. By WILLIAM TALLACK. With Portrait, cloth, 2s. 6d.

---

**ILLUSTRATED PENNY READINGS:**
being Twelve separate Readings by various Authors. Bound in cloth, 1s. 6d.; in packets or paper covers, 1s. each.

---

**THE FOUR PILLARS OF TEMPER-**
ANCE. By J. W. KIRTON, Author of "*Buy your own Cherries.*" With an Engraving, cloth, 1s. 6d. Paper cover, 1s.

---

**THE BREWER'S FAMILY;** *or, Experi-*
ences of Charles Crawford. By Mrs. ELLIS. With EIGHT Engravings, cloth, 2s. 6d.

---

**MARIE & THE SEVEN CHILDREN.**
A Tale for Elder Girls. By Mrs. GELDART. With TEN Engravings, cloth, 1s.

---

London: S. W PARTRIDGE, 9, Paternoster Row.

# Story of Two Apprentices:

The Dishonest and The Successful. By the Rev. J. T. BARR. With FOUR Engravings, 6d.

"The 'Two Apprentices' should be put into every boy's hands; they will be sure to read it, and cannot fail of learning some valuable lessons from its pages. It is more natural and true than Hogarth's Two Apprentices."—*Wesleyan Times.*  [*Tenth Thousand.*

---

# Hannah Twift:

A Story about Temper. By Miss BAKEWELL. With Two Engravings, 6d.

"Hannah Twift is a young servant girl unfortunately possessing a bad temper, which gets her into all kinds of difficulties, even from childhood; and ultimately is the secondary cause of her being apprehended on the charge of murdering the aunt of her mistress, for which she is tried and found guilty, and sentenced to die."—*Art Journal.*

---

# Philip Markham's Two Leffons.

By Author of "Dick and his Donkey." With FOUR Engravings, 6d.

"Philip Markham is the title of an interesting story of one who was wilful and proud. Like Solomon's 'foolish son,' he was more than once a 'heaviness to his mother.' But he learnt obedience through suffering. His two lessons were dearly bought, but in the end worth more than they cost."—*Glasgow Christian News.*

---

# Scrub;

Or, the Workhouse Boy's First Start in Life. By Mrs. BALFOUR. With SEVEN Engravings, 6d.

This interesting narrative of a poor London Workhouse boy, illustrates in a most striking manner the value of "right principles," especially of honesty, truthfulness, and sobriety. It is a suitable present for apprentices, and the senior scholars in Sunday Schools.
[*Twentieth Thousand.*

---

# The Rod, and its Ufes;

Or, Thomas Dodd and Bill Collins. By Author of "My Flowers." With FIVE Engravings, 6d.

CONTENTS:—A Sketch of Dodd's Family Management and its Consequences—A Clergyman's Difficulties—Dodd feels his own Faultiness, and suffers for it—First Misfortune—First Comfort and Second Trouble—A Stubborn Son refuses Good Advice—Collins's Cottage: a Peep into its Politics—The Secret of Collins's Happiness—The Hounds and the Whipper-in—Sorrow upon Sorrow—Effects of Strong Drink—Friends indeed—Comfort and Encouragement—Darkness and Day-dawn.

---

London: S. W. PARTRIDGE, 9, Paternoster Row.

## THE DAIRYMAN'S DAUGHTER: an

Authentic Narrative. By the Rev. LEGH RICHMOND, M.A. With TWENTY Engravings, cloth, 1s. 6d.; gilt, 2s. 6d.

---

## COME HOME, MOTHER! A Story for

Mothers. By NELSIE BROOK. With TEN Engravings, cloth, 1s.

---

## MAUDE'S VISIT TO SANDY BEACH.

A Book for Girls. By the Author of "Croffes of Childhood." With FOUR Engravings, cloth, 1s.

---

## PROCRASTINATING MARY. A Story

for Young Girls. By the Author of "Croffes of Childhood." With TWO Engravings, 6d.

---

## ROSA; or, The Two Caftles. By Mifs

BRADBURN. A Tale for Girls. With EIGHT Engravings, cloth, 1s.
[New Edition.

---

## PASSAGES IN THE HISTORY OF A

SHILLING. By Mrs. C. L. BALFOUR. With FIVE Engravings, cloth, 1s.
[New Edition.

---

## OUR DUMB COMPANIONS; or, Stories

about Dogs, Horfes, Cats, and Donkeys. By Rev. T. JACKSON, M.A. With SEVENTY-FIVE Engravings, cloth, 5s; gilt, 7s. 6d. [Eighth Thoufand.

---

## THE LITTLE WOODMAN & HIS

DOG CÆSAR. By Mrs. SHERWOOD. Parlour Iffue on toned paper, cloth, 1s. 6d.; gilt, 2s. 6d. [New Edition.

---

## WASTE NOT, WANT NOT. A Book

for Servants. By Mrs. SHERWOOD. Printed on toned paper, cloth, 1s. 6d.; gilt, 2s. 6d. [New Edition.

---

London: S. W. PARTRIDGE, 9, Paternofter Row.

## THE MOTHER'S PICTURE ALPHA-

BET. Printed on Toned Paper. With TWENTY-SIX Engravings, boards, 5s.; cloth, red edges, 7s. 6d.; gilt edges, 10s. 6d. [*Seventh Thousand.*]

---

## A MOTHER'S LESSONS ON THE

LORD'S PRAYER. By Mrs. BALFOUR. With EIGHT Engravings, illustrated cover, 2s. 6d.; cloth, 3s. 6d.; cloth extra, 5s.

---

## A MOTHER'S STORIES FOR HER

CHILDREN. By Mrs. CARUS WILSON. With FOUR Engravings, cloth, 1s. [*New Edition.*]

---

## A MOTHER'S LESSONS ON KIND-

NESS TO ANIMALS. With FORTY-THREE Engravings, 2 vols., cloth, 1s. each.

---

## THE GOVERNESS; or, the Missing Pencil-

Case. By the Rev. J. T. BARR. With TWELVE Engravings, cloth, 1s. [*Fifteenth Thousand.*]

---

## RACHEL; or, Little Faults. By Charlotte

ELIZABETH. With SEVEN Engravings, cloth, 1s. [*Ninth Thousand.*]

---

## THE GIANTS; and How to Fight Them.

By Dr. NEWTON. With EIGHT Engravings, cloth, 1s. [*Ninth Thousand.*]

---

## THE PRINCE CONSORT: His Life and

Character. By the Rev. J. H. WILSON. With SIX Engravings, cloth, 1s. [*Twenty-first Thousand.*]

---

## COUSIN BESSIE: a Story of Youthful

Earnestness. By Mrs. BALFOUR. With EIGHT Engravings, cloth, 1s. [*Tenth Thousand.*]

---

London: S. W. PARTRIDGE, 9, Paternoster Row.

# THREE OPPORTUNITIES; or, the Story

of Henry Forrefter. With EIGHT Engravings, cloth, 2s. 6d.

---

# CROSSES OF CHILDHOOD; or, Little

Alice and Her Friends. By Mrs. WALLER. With FIVE Engravings, cloth, 1s.

---

# THE CHILDREN'S PARTY; or, a Day

at Upland. Being Stories in Profe and Verfe. By COUSIN HELEN. With SIX Engravings, cloth, 1s.

---

# SONGS AND HYMNS FOR THE

LITTLE ONES. Compiled by UNCLE JOHN. With ONE HUNDRED AND SIXTY Engravings, cloth, 5s.; coloured plates and gilt edges, 7s. 6d.

---

# MORNING DEW-DROPS; or, the Ju-

venile Abftainer. By Mrs. C. L. BALFOUR. With SIXTEEN Engravings, cloth, 3s. 6d.; gilt, 4s. 6d.                              [*Fifth Edition.*

---

# TOIL AND TRUST; or, Life-Story of

Patty, the Workhoufe Girl. By Mrs. BALFOUR. With FOUR Engravings, cloth, 1s.                              [*Twelfth Thoufand.*

---

# FAMILY WALKING-STICKS; or, Profe

Portraits of my Relations. By GEORGE MOGRIDGE (Old Humphrey), with a Preface by his Widow. With EIGHT Engravings, cloth, 1s. 6d.

---

# THE SICK ROOM AND ITS SECRET.

By Mrs. THOMAS GELDART. With TWENTY-TWO Engravings, cloth, 1s.

---

# TOM BURTON: a Tale of the Workfhop.

By the Author of "The Working Man's Way in the World." With SIX Engravings, cloth, 1s.                              [*Tenth Thoufand.*

---

London: S. W. PARTRIDGE, 9, Paternofter Row.

*JOHN TODD, and How he Stirred his Own*
Broth-Pot. By the Rev. JOHN ALLAN. With FOUR Engravings, cloth, 1s.

---

*THOUGHTS FOR YOUNG THINKERS.*
By AARON HALL (Old Humphrey). With TWENTY-NINE Engravings,
cloth, 1s. [*Tenth Thousand.*

---

*CLUB NIGHT: a Village Record. Edited*
by C. L BALFOUR. With TWELVE Engravings, cloth, 1s.

---

*DOMESTIC ADDRESSES, and Scraps of*
Experience. By G. MOGRIDGE (Old Humphrey). With TWENTY-THREE
Engravings, cloth, 1s. 6d.

---

*WANDERINGS OF A BIBLE: and My*
Mother's Bible. By Mrs. BALFOUR. With EIGHT Engravings, cloth, 1s.
[*Tenth Thousand.*

---

*JOHN HOBBS: a Temperance Tale of*
Britiſh India. By GEORGE DRAGO. With TWELVE Engravings, cloth, 1s.
[*Tenth Thousand.*

---

*OUR MORAL WASTES, and How to Re-*
claim Them. By Rev. J. H. WILSON. With FOUR Engravings, cloth, 1s.
[*Second Edition.*

---

*SUNDAY SCHOOL ILLUSTRATIONS.*
By EPHRAIM HOLDING (Old Humphrey). With THIRTY-NINE Engravings,
cloth, 1s. 6d.

---

*HOMELY HINTS ON HOUSEHOLD*
MANAGEMENT. By Mrs. C. L. BALFOUR. With TWENTY-TWO
Engravings, cloth, 1s. [*Tenth Thousand.*

---

London: S. W. PARTRIDGE, 9, Paternoſter Row.

*NANCY WIMBLE, the Village Goſſip, and*
How ſhe was Cured. By T. S. ARTHUR. With EIGHT Engravings, cloth, 1s. 6d.

---

*THE HAUNTED HOUSE; or, Dark*
Paſſages in the Life of Dora Langley. By ELIZA S. OLDHAM. With FOUR Engravings, cloth, 1s.

---

*MIND WHOM YOU MARRY; or, the*
Gardener's Daughter. By the Rev. C. G. ROWE. With EIGHT Engravings, cloth, 1s.　　　　　　　　　　　　[*Twentieth Thouſand.*

---

*HOW FAMILIES ARE RENDERED*
HAPPY OR MISERABLE. By UNCLE DAVID. With THIRTY-FOUR Engravings, cloth, 1s.

---

*WHAT PUT MY PIPE OUT; or, Inci-*
dents in the Life of a Clergyman. Illuſtrated by GEORGE CRUIKSHANK. With FIVE Engravings, cloth, 1s. 6d.

---

*WILLY HEATH AND THE HOUSE*
RENT. By WILLIAM LEASK, D.D. With TEN Engravings, cloth, 1s. 6d.

---

*GOOD SERVANTS, GOOD WIVES, &*
HAPPY HOMES. By the Rev. T. H. WALKER. With FOURTEEN Engravings, cloth, 1s. 6d.　　　　　　　　　[*Tenth Thouſand.*

---

*RAINY DAYS, and How to Meet Them.*
By Mrs. MARSHALL. With FOUR Engravings, cloth, 1s.

---

*WIDOW GREEN AND HER THREE*
NIECES. By Mrs ELLIS. With TWENTY-FOUR Engravings, cloth, 1s.　　　　　　　　　　　[*Thirty-eighth Thouſand.*

---

London : S. W. PARTRIDGE, 9, Paternoſter Row.

# Nettie Leigh's Birthday.

By A. E. R.   With FIVE Engravings, 6d.

CONTENTS :—The Pine-cone Basket and the Sunbeams—The Drive to the Wood—The Ruins—Muff and the Hedgehog—The Owl in the Tower—The Lame Girl and the Cottage—A Disaster—The Coronation—Good Resolutions—Nettie and Minnie going Home —" Good Night, and Pleasant Dreams."

# Joseph Selden, the Cripple;

Or, an Angel in our Home.   By the Author of "The Dalrymples."   With FIVE Engravings, 6d.

CONTENTS :—A Peep into John Selden's Home—Joey the Cripple—His Patience and Endurance—A Comfort to his Mother—Timely Aid—Bitter Reflections—John Selden in search of Employment—Settles at the Isle of Wight—Joey a Cripple for Life—Is carried to the Beach—A Lady Visitor—Promise of a Bible—Bookmarkers—The Happy Transformation—Joey does what he can for Missions—Is made a Blessing—He Sickens and Dies.

# Friends of the Friendless;

Or, a Few Chapters from Prison Life.   By Mrs. BALFOUR.   With NINE Engravings, 6d.

" Short sketches of philanthropists, chiefly in humble life, well adapted to incite the possessors of a single talent to turn it to good account, by showing what the *poor have been able to do for the poor*."—*Englishwoman's Journal*.

# Pity the Little Ones!

Or, Little Ellen the Gleaner.   By the Author of "Haunted House."   With Two Engravings, 6d.

" We should think it would be almost impossible for any one to read this graphic sketch of the drunkard's home and child, without being moved with pity and sympathy for the little ones.   We would earnestly recommend parents and Sabbath-school teachers to purchase and carefully read this interesting narrative."—*Maidstone Temperance Visitor*.

# How Sam Adams' Pipe became a Pig.

By J. W. KIRTON, Author of " Buy your own Cherries."   With FIVE Engravings by Cruikshank.

CONTENTS :—How Sam loved his Pipe, and how he went to see the Wild Beasts—How Mr. Wombwell objected to Smoking, because it taught the Monkeys Bad Habits—Sam burns his Idol, and his Clothes from off his Back—Dr. Prout's opinion of the Weed—Little Pigs with Straws in their mouths—Charley puts a very awkward question—Sam becomes thoughtful, especially when his wife calls him a " Walking Chimey-pot"—Self-conquest and Victory.

London : S. W. PARTRIDGE, 9, Paternoster Row.

# BIBLE PRINTS: a Series of Twenty-four

beautifully Tinted Engravings, illuftrative of the Old and New Teftaments. By Profeffor SCHNORR. With Explanatory Letterprefs by the Rev. JOHN ROSE, B.D., and the Rev. J. W. BURGON, M.A. With TWENTY-FOUR Engravings, paper covers, 4s.

---

# A VOICE FROM THE VINTAGE; or,

the Force of Example. By Mrs. ELLIS. Crown 8vo., cloth, 1s.

[Fourth Edition.

---

# TRUTH FRAE' MANG THE HEATHER;

or, Is the Bible True? By a WORKING MAN. With SIX Engravings, cloth, 1s.

[Fourth Thoufand.

---

# HAVE WE ANY WORD OF GOD?

The Queftion of the Day. By the Author of " Is the Bible True?" With SEVEN Engravings, cloth, 1s.

---

# THE TWO CHRISTMAS DAYS. THE

CHRISTMAS BOX. By Mrs. BALFOUR. With FIVE Engravings, cloth, 1s.

---

# THE CHRISTIAN MONITOR; or, Selec-

tions from Pious Authors. With Fifty Engravings, cloth, 2s. 6d.; cloth, gilt edges, 3s. 6d.

---

# ILLUSTRATED HANDBILLS, for

General Diftribution. With EIGHTY-THREE Engravings, 8vo., cloth, and in packets, 1s. each. Each Handbill may alfo be had feparate, in SIXPENNY Packets, afforted or otherwife.

---

# TRACTS FOR THE SUPPRESSION OF

INTEMPERANCE. In afforted packets. Many Engravings, 1s.

---

London: S. W. PARTRIDGE, 9, Paternofter Row.

www.ingramcontent.com/pod-product-compliance
Lightning Source LLC
Chambersburg PA
CBHW031106020726
47495CB00007B/2077